WESLEYAN VILE-TALITY

RECLAIMING THE HEART OF METHODIST IDENTITY

ASHLEY BOGGAN

Abingdon Press | Nashville

WESLEYAN VILE-TALITY
RECLAIMING THE HEART OF METHODIST IDENTITY

Library of Congress Control Number: 2025932217
ISBN 978-1-7910-3941-7

MANUFACTURED IN THE UNITED STATES OF AMERICA

For mama:
Rev. Rebecca Boggan (1955–2022)

For daddy:
Rev. Dr. William Kurt Boggan (1954–2022)

Y'all's ministries live on.
Love you both.

(And a special thanks to Bottle Hill Tavern
in Madison, New Jersey. Thanks for
providing an inspirational place to write.)

CONTENTS

PREFACE

Within the Christian tradition, being Wesleyan and/or Methodist calls us to actively stand as a beacon of justice in this world. You cannot identify as Wesleyan or Methodist without constantly seeking to ensure that all people, no matter who they are, how they identify, or where they come from, feel worthy of God's love, have their basic physical and bodily needs met, and have the ability to seek happiness and perfection in Jesus Christ. If we are actually living into this call of our faith, this book will argue that we will be known as a people who bend the rules and push the boundaries of society to ensure God's love is continuously felt.

This is the core aspect of our identity, one that we've lost, and one that we need to claim. It can be summed up in the ideology of Wesleyan vile-tality—a willingness to look beyond today's acceptable practices, standards, and norms and bend the rules in order to ensure that more and more persons can be included within the Kin-dom of God. And also that all persons, no matter who they are, how they identify, whom they love, or how they live can know and experience the love of God, can know their own self-worth, and can grow to love themselves so that they can love others.

This book will delve into the foundational stories of our Wesleyan/ Methodist history and connect them to our current moment within

The United Methodist Church (UMC). John Wesley set out to revive the Church of England toward a renewed sense of mission and faith acted out as love. How can we, as United Methodists, seek to reform ourselves to, once again, be a beacon of embodied loving justice in a world that is increasingly polarized? Together, we will journey through the life of John Wesley and those early Methodists, discovering their unwavering commitment to spreading the gospel to the marginalized and their relentless pursuit of social justice. We will also see the contexts for and the consequences of becoming an institutionalized church that lost some of that rule-bending Spirit. The main question this book will leave you with is, "What is our identity moving forward?"

This book is an analysis of our identities as Methodists throughout history. It will delve into our past, but I promise it'll be an approachable, fun trip backwards that propels us forward with stories of resurrection and of rebirth of a church identity. As you read, I invite you to open your mind to the radicalness of John Wesley and those early Methodists. As we examine how their identities formed, how their faith shaped a movement, and how that movement became an institution, I invite you to think of your faith journey. Why are you Wesleyan, Methodist, and/or United Methodist? What DNA from those early folks still lingers inside of us? What pieces might we need to leave behind? What pieces might need to be reclaimed?

1

THE CALL TO WESLEYAN VILE-TALITY

In Death There Is Resurrection

The first time I visited the Wesley heritage sites in England, I was sixteen years old. I was traveling with my family to visit my sister, who was spending a semester studying abroad at Oxford University. My mother and father—who were both ordained clergy in The UMC—dragged me to City Road, and we looked at John Wesley's grave through a fence. I remember pulling on my dad's shirt and saying, "Why are we looking at some dead guy's grave?" Little did I know that within a decade, I'd be seeking a PhD studying *that* dead guy.

It would be twenty years before I returned to these sites but with a new, more appreciative lens. In the summer of 2022, I had the immense privilege to travel with other Metho-nerds on the Wesley

Pilgrimage hosted by Discipleship Ministries. It was led by Rev. Dr. Paul Chilcote, Rev. Dr. Steve Manskar, and Rev. Melanie Gordon. For this trip, I put on my pilgrim hat; I was going as a United Methodist laywoman, as a person in need of spiritual renewal—not as a scholar, and definitely not as a general secretary. I was there to learn, not teach. I was excited about seeing London and walking down Aldersgate Street where John had his heart strangely warmed. In Oxford, I was anxious to get to Christ Church and see the pulpit from which Wesley preached. And I couldn't believe that we would get to go to Epworth and see the home where John Wesley was raised and sit at *the* table where Susanna taught her children. However, I was not as excited about Bristol; in all honesty, I really couldn't remember what happened in Bristol. But little did I know that I would have a similar experience in Bristol to that of John Wesley—it would change everything.

Arriving at the seaport town of Bristol, we got off the coach and walked down what seemed like an outdoor mall. I couldn't help but think, *Where are we going?* And in the middle of these shops, tucked back from the main walkway, was an unassuming white building. It had a large statue in front of it with John Wesley on horseback, and honestly, without this statue, I might have walked right by it.

We walked inside and wow! The stark white of the plaster walls contrasted with the wooden pews, benches, and pulpit. Its interior screamed old Methodist. All of the pilgrims wandered around a bit before finding our seats in the (nineteenth-century, not original) pews. I sat next to a person who would become a true friend, Rev. Chris Heckert. Into the main room walked a joyful British man, David Worthington. He welcomed us and started talking about all of the Methodist things that happened in Bristol. As he was talking, I started remembering how crucial Bristol was to the Wesleys. How could I have forgotten?

2

As David talked, I began to remember the revival in Bristol of 1739, and I began to vaguely recall that Wesley did something for the first time in this place. And that's when David read from John Wesley's journal. And it all came rushing back. But it came rushing back in a renewed way, a way that suddenly made everything make sense. My mind began racing as I listened and I kept thinking, *There's something about this place that's different. There's a message here that we all need.* David read from John's journal...

> *Saturday [March] 31, [1739]*
> In the evening, I reached Bristol, and met Mr. Whitefield there. I could scarce reconcile myself at first to this strange way of preaching in the fields...having been all my life (till very lately) so tenacious of every point relating to decency and order, that I should've thought the saving of souls a sin if it had not been done inside of a church.

> *[Sunday] April 1, [1739]*
> In the evening (Mr. Whitefield being gone) I begun expounding our Lord's Sermon on the Mount, (one pretty remarkable precedent of field preaching, though I suppose there were churches at that time also) to a little society which was accustomed to meet once or twice a week in Nicholas Street.

> *Monday [April] 2, [1739]*
> At four o'clock in the afternoon, I submitted to be more vile, and preaching the glad tidings of salvation from a little eminence in a ground adjoining to the city to about three thousand people.

There was so much to unpack in those words, but what kept repeating in my head, and the phrase that David Worthington read twice was "submitted to be more vile."

Submitted. To. Be. More. Vile.

Submitted.

Vile.

I'd heard or read this journal entry from April 2, 1739, probably a dozen times. It never hit me the same way as it did sitting there in the New Room, in Bristol, hearing John's words read by a guy with a British accent.

When David finished with his talk, we all got up, got our pictures preaching from the pulpit, toured the (amazing!) museum, and left. But Bristol wouldn't leave me alone. Something changed there for me. And I couldn't get David's voice out of my head—*be more vile.* Some of us pilgrims gathered at a pub later that night, and we all agreed that Bristol was our favorite stop on the pilgrimage. It was the first Methodist preaching house—the first Methodist building in the world! And it's where John Wesley's entire ministry changed. Little did I know it's where my entire ministry would change, too.

A few days later, through tears, all the pilgrims hugged each other and said goodbye—as if we'd never see each other again despite our all being very involved in the UM connection. And I boarded my plane. When I landed back in New Jersey, my life changed—but not for the better.

You see, my parents lived back in Arkansas. In February of 2020, right before everything shut down due to COVID-19, my mom (who was my best friend) had a brain bleed. Two months later—in the middle of the shutdown—she had another. After her second one, she was unable to communicate either through speech or writing. After being discharged from one month of rehab (where, because of COVID restrictions, we couldn't see her at all), she had aged what looked like thirty years. Where a strong-willed, funny, wise woman once sat was now a frail, confused person. She was gone. She was physically here, but she was gone. She was alive, but my mom, my best friend, was gone.

With the ongoing shutdown, my father stayed home through the rest of 2020, all of 2021, and into 2022, and he cared for her 24/7. He refused help (stubbornness runs deep in my DNA). In fact, for Christmas 2021, I gifted him a spot on the Wesley Pilgrimage—I guess I felt like I needed to apologize for pulling him away from Wesley's grave all those years before. But with Mom sick, he felt like he couldn't leave. He wouldn't be able to enjoy the history or sites with his mind back on her at home. So, he stayed in Arkansas caring for Mom, and I flew to England.

When I landed after the pilgrimage in July 2022, I immediately called him. I had to tell him about all of the things I had seen, and I had to tell him about Bristol. I knew he'd roll his eyes in a loving, proud manner when I began to rant about "be more vile." But he'd listen because he always did. He was one of the few people—at that time at least—with whom I could truly Metho-nerd out. He didn't answer, but I didn't think anything of it. It was late, after all. The next morning, I tried again. Still no answer. I called my sister, who was with her family at Disney World. "Hey, I'm back. Have you talked to Dad? He's not answering?"

"Yeah, I talked to him yesterday. He had COVID last week and didn't sound great, but he's no longer testing positive. I'll call the neighbor and see if he can go over and check." The neighbor knocked on his door, but there was no answer.

I ended up calling the police to do a wellness check. I remember that moment, hearing those words as if they weren't actually coming out of the phone: "Ma'am, I don't know how to tell you this, but he's dead." I don't know what else the police officer said after that; I just remember collapsing. Eventually I heard him asking, "Is someone else here with your father?"

And then I came to again, "Yes, my mother. She's on hospice and cannot communicate. Is she ok?"

"She's still nicely tucked in bed, but she's awake."

Mom lived another three months after Dad died. It was the exact time that the doctor had given her to live back in April of 2020. But with Dad's loving care, she "lived" for an unexpected two and a half years. But within three months, they were both gone. My world turned completely upside down. And I threw all of my grief into my work (which my therapist assured me was a healthy outlet).

Be. More. Vile.

Even in the midst of all of this grief, I still couldn't get those three words out of my head. Luckily, after the pilgrimage, I had stayed in touch with three of the pilgrims. We had even branded ourselves the More Vile Methodist Network. They helped me process grief, provided needed memes, and were my go-to space to Metho-nerd out.

Wrestling with Wesley's journal entry from April 2 seemed to be healing for me. God works in weird ways. As a Christian people, we are called to believe that in death there is life. And when you think about it, what could be more "vile" than Jesus's resurrection? In fact, when you really think about it, who better an example of a "vile" person than Jesus? I know I just insinuated that Jesus is vile, but please don't shut the book yet. Give me a moment. Think of all the socially-upending, physics-defying, and rule-bending aspects of his life and ministry. He dared to claim that the rich shall be last and the poor shall be first. He associated with tax collectors and women who had been cast aside. And my personal favorite, he turned water into wine! All of this was so abhorrent to the Roman government that it sanctioned his killing in the lowliest form of execution possible: crucifixion. And then he had the *vile* audacity to defy death. His story lived on; his ministry and witness lived on as others embodied his call to be a witness for and to all in this world. In my parents' death, a new journey of faith opened up for me, a new calling to help others reclaim the authentic Wesleyan identity in which they raised me. Their ministries were cut short, but it felt healing to carry their witness, their understanding of Wesley forward—for in death, there is life.

I cannot help but connect the parallels of my own trauma between 2020 and 2023 with the traumatic experiences within The United Methodist Church. After the General Conference of 2019, and with the onset of COVID-19, The UMC was forced into a period of waiting with bated breath, wondering when, how, and to what end it was going to gather next. During this time, the trust clause was shattered, covenants were broken, and some congregations left. The UMC experienced its own grief and identity crisis. And now it's time that we be reminded of who we really were, are, and could be again, *for in death, there is life.* We have a chance to be reborn, to resurrect our true selves, to tell our stories anew. The hard part of doing this, however, is that not everyone likes what I believe to be the true, dare I say "orthodox," perspective of Wesley and the reputation of the people called Methodist. Our true identity claims us as rabble-rousers, outsiders, and rule-benders and blatantly calls us to "be more vile." For the affirming theology that Wesley preached and the ways that those early Methodists pushed the confined boundaries of church and state, they were beaten, jailed, harassed, and disowned. Again, this has a very close parallel to those early Christians. For telling the story of a resurrected Jesus, they were persecuted, jailed, martyred, and cast out. But that didn't stop them. Those early Methodists didn't stop either... at least for a bit. Embracing our core identity requires a deep faith, a deep commitment to the very idea that God can do anything and all if we are willing to submit to God's call for us—even if that calls us to new fields.

Coming out of this parallel trauma, and putting back on my scholarly historian and general secretary hat, I hope that the stories throughout this book help us collectively move on and reclaim our identity and lead us toward a Pentecost, one that might signal a rebirth of The United Methodist Church as a connection that has, once again, found its willingness to be a bit more vile. After all, it was on Pentecost that John Wesley famously felt his heart "strangely warmed." Might The UMC seek a similar moment of renewal and open our hearts, once again, to the strangely warm inner workings of God.

For Wesley, It All Changed in Bristol

Typically, when Methodist scholars speak of Methodist history, we begin with the "three rises" of Methodism. This was, after all, how John Wesley himself described the beginnings of the movement. But, if you ask me, Methodism doesn't start with Oxford, Georgia, or London—yes, it has crucial components that were formed in those spaces, and John's faith and mission were shaped by the particularities of certain experiences in these three rises, but John Wesley didn't really figure out what his true calling was, what he was doing (or how or why), until Bristol.

Let's set the stage. It's winter 1738, and John Wesley was in London, having had his heart "strangely warmed" early that May. Charles, his younger brother, had a similar experience ("a strange palpitation of his heart") *three days prior* (sibling rivalry is an age-old custom!). Charles was working with James Hutton to reshape a religious society more toward a Moravian understanding of faith—one focused on God's all-assuring love. After Georgia, John was in

Germany with a friend, Benjamin Ingham while George Whitefield, a fellow Methodist leader (although of a more Calvinist bent), was preaching in the American colonies. But that New Year's Eve of 1738, the OG Holy Club—the spiritual formation group that John had started in college some ten years earlier—reunited, exchanged ministry stories, and attended a Moravian watch-night service. During this service, the seven old Oxford buddies had a collective Pentecost experience—a call from the Holy Spirit to reform the Church of England from the inside out. After this, they returned to their respective corners of England and brought a more evangelical flair to their preaching.[1]

Now *evangelical* in this sense does not mean the same thing that we think of in 2025. The evangelical voting bloc or nondenominationalist rise in the 1970s and forward is an entirely different theology and ideology. In the eighteenth century, evangelical meant an emphasis on four things: on initiating a conversion experience, on Scripture as authoritative guide for life, on the work of Jesus Christ on the cross, and on testimony of the heart changed.[2] These four things, especially combined, could have been transformative for the eighteenth-century Anglican faith, which predominately relied upon static (sometimes sleeping) butts in the pews on Sunday morning and not necessarily the active working of the Holy Spirit in and through us every day.

Opposite of this, the "evangelicals" of the eighteenth century tended to speak more to the heart than the brain. They tended to use language that was body-centric and spoke of how God or the Spirit would affect you internally. Evangelical sermons were evocative, emotional, energetic. They spoke of Jesus's body and its suffering on the cross. And then they encouraged you, the listener, to act on these newfound feelings—either seeking to convert others or seeking to change the world by living out your love of God.

9

Action? How radical were these evangelicals? Faith should cause one to act? Faith acted out as love? This, combined with the assurance of God's love (the idea that we can all *know* that we are *all* loved by God), meant that evangelicals walked around all "happy in God" for the love of God had "cast out all fear," and so they could rejoice. For this (weird) happiness, they were labeled "enthusiasts" and were seen as borderline "dissenters."

After this fateful reunion on New Year's Eve, four of the seven OG Holy Clubbers had pulpits to return to and preach this evangelical message. But John Wesley, Charles Wesley, and George Whitefield did not have pulpits—they preached only by invitation. Throughout the winter of 1738 and 1739, these three preachers began to be cast out from the institutional church for their radical message of God's love and their expectation of an emotional response. For example, Charles Wesley decided to preach against a public hanging and brought a message of God's love to the town of Tyburn as witness to the execution. By doing this, Charles actually preached outdoors a few months prior to his brother! (Again, sibling rivalry!) Charles did not enjoy preaching outdoors, and particularly the pushback he received for so doing, and he advised John to *never* do such a thing. George Whitefield had long been known to be an overly dramatic preacher—he was quite loud, had crossed eyes, and used his hands probably too much while he spoke (one can imagine John Wesley's rules for preaching as antithetical to the style of Whitefield). And John was getting too comfortable, theologically and missionally, with the Moravians (who were already labeled dissenters).

The three of them together were focusing on forming religious societies, which only fueled the suspicion of dissent and potential enthusiastic unrest. The Fetter Lane Society in London was their main project that winter. This society was comprised predominately of German Moravians and French Huguenots who functioned as their guinea pigs for new theologies and a base from which they could train new leaders.[3] It was from leading this society in London that George and, afterwards, John headed to Bristol.

After being ordained a presbyter, George Whitefield decided to spend February 1739 in Bristol. According to preeminent British Methodist historian G. M. Best, Bristol was more ripe for religious enthusiasm and reform, as the city had a number of already active religious societies and a decently-sized dissenting population. Bristol was the second largest city in England at the time, just behind London. It was filthy; some would call it the dirtiest city in all of Europe. It was run by a select few oligarchs who controlled its industry and massive shipping operations. It is from Bristol that all exports were shipped out and all imports came in—including enslaved people and the commodities of their enslaved labor. Within a few decades it would be the birthplace of the Industrial Revolution. In order to better understand the place where Methodism was birthed, it's worth quoting G. M. Best at length:

> The priority of the merchant-run city authorities was largely to ensure ever-increasing profits rather than to care for the workforce. Most workers were paid wages that scarce enabled them to live and their families lived a day-to-day hand-to-mouth existence. Many drowned their sorrows in cheap alcohol and in the poorest areas every tenth house was an alehouse. Brutality and crime were therefore commonplace. So too was disease because, in the absence of any sewage system, an open drain ran down each street and, whenever it rained, some of its contents flowed into either the River Aron or the River Frome, so polluting the city's main sources of drinking water. Into these drains were thrown not just urine and excrement from humans and animals but the unwanted byproducts from the city's manufacturers

and slaughterhouses. The resulting foul mess clogged the streets, rendering wheeled vehicles so inoperable that traders had to use iron-shod sledges to carry goods across the city.[4]

Traditionally, preachers who visited various towns (or dioceses) across England were to get the permission of the appropriate bishop prior to accepting a preaching invitation. Whitefield wrote to the bishop for permission, but he didn't await an answer. Instead, doing as the Holy Club had done in Oxford, Whitefield preached at Newgate Prison. He preached inside of parishes, in rented spaces to societies, and in coal mining fields outdoors. Within the first month, he was preaching thirty times each week to tens of thousands of people (apparently, another universal trend in history is the tendency for preachers to inflate numbers).

With all of this spiritual excitement, Whitefield was beginning to feel burnt-out, and he was feeling called to preach in the American colonies again. But he couldn't just leave these burgeoning societies high and dry. So, he started writing people asking for help. And, well, John was not his first choice. His first was actually Charles Wesley (sibling rivalry again!). John was not even his second choice, but his fifth. He writes to John, "There is a glorious door opened among the colliers. You must come and water what God has enabled me to plant."[5] George then made an appeal for John's organizational expertise in order to fully woo him to Bristol. While Charles warned John not to go, John seemed intrigued. He wrote a letter to his friend (and OG Holy Clubber) John Clayton: "I look upon all the world as my parish.... In whatever part of it I am, I judge it meet, right, and my bound duty to declare unto all that are willing to hear the glad tidings of salvation. This is the work which I know God has called me to do."[6] But, John being John, he turned to Scripture before making a final decision. He opened his Bible four times to see what God might tell him (I guess the first three answers weren't what he was looking for). He doesn't record which Scripture appeared nor what it said, but he left London for Bristol.

On March 31, 1739, the day of his arrival, John saw Whitefield preach for the first time; but he was not preaching inside a church (as John had expected him to be). He was preaching in the fields of Bristol, specifically to coal miners gathered there. John writes in his journal, "I scarcely could reconcile myself at first to this strange way of preaching in the fields." Now, at least for me, when I think of early Methodism, I tend to go directly to preaching in the fields—to camp meetings, to revivals, to John's preaching atop his father's grave. But those are all moments that happen *after* Bristol. Up until this point, John had followed the preaching standards of his day: "I had been all my life (till very lately) so tenacious of every point relating to decency and order that I should have thought the saving of souls almost a sin if it had not been done in a church."[7]

On April 2, 1739, only two days after his arrival, he does something he never thought he would: "At four in the afternoon, I submitted to be more vile and proclaimed in the highways the glad tidings of salvation, speaking from a little eminence in a ground adjoining to the city, to about three thousand people."[8]

Submitted. This word is used intentionally. John did not want to do this. But he felt called by the Holy Spirit to go into the fields, to the people who had yet to hear the love of God. Outdoor preaching was reminiscent of the days of "enthusiasm" when so-called religious fanatics threatened the monarchy. The Methodists were already seen as a bit "enthusiastic" but had yet to really cause so much of a stir as to get noticed. But preaching outdoors, *that* might get attention—and not the kind John wanted. But he did it anyway. Why? Because God called him to go to Bristol and he saw the missional need; he saw people in need of a message of love, and he saw the effect

13

Whitefield was having on them. He couldn't resist the Spirit, and so he submitted to it.

Vile—let's deal with that word, too. When we hear this word in its adjective form, we tend to think of something or someone dirty, disgusting, unseemly—and this is probably what was on Wesley's mind when he recalled beginning to preach in fields and elsewhere in his journal. He was still very much an Oxford don, raised in the upper echelons of British society and highly educated, and while he didn't keep much money to his name, no one would dare think of Wesley as a person without means. He was, despite his objections later in life, a part of the "proper British society." As an ordained clergyperson and an Oxford fellow, he represented the state, the church, and the educated elite. And yet, here he was, about to preach in a field to some of the poorest folks in all of England from one of the dirtiest towns in the Western world. And while John didn't want to do this, he definitely didn't want to do it in a space that was so filthy—thus, "vile" seemed accurate.

Vile can also be an adverb; it can describe certain actions as morally reprehensible, against the standards of society. In this sense of the word, John was knowingly violating decorum. He was not only putting himself in a place that was "vile" but was acting in a way that he considered to be "vile." He even described how he had previously felt about saving souls outside the church—at one time in his life he had considered it sinful to save someone not within a church. But here he was, again, called to be vile. Called to go to where people were in need and awaken the Spirit of God within them—even if it wasn't inside of a church.

Wesley also probably used this word in an adverbial sense because he knew that *this* act might garner some negative attention, specifically from the bishop of Bristol. And he was right. The bishop inquired rather quickly after word got around that Wesley was preaching in Bristol, outdoors. Wesley received a letter from the bishop inquiring as to why he's preaching in Bristol at all, let alone outdoors. As it is in today's connection, it was common courtesy for an ordained minister to let a bishop know if they were going to be within the confines of, or especially preaching within, their diocese. Wesley hadn't done that. So, the bishop insists, "You have no business here. You are not commissioned to preach in this diocese. Therefore, I advise you to go hence."

In response, Wesley lays out what he meant by the words he had written previously to his friend John Clayton: "I look upon all the world as my parish." He responds, "My Lord, my business on earth is, to do what good I can. Wherever, therefore, I think I can do most good, there must I stay, so long as I think so. At present I think I can do most good here; therefore, here I stay." With this response, Wesley was stating that following the call of God or the movement of the Holy Spirit cannot be confined by the boundaries of a region, the walls of a church, or the rules of an institution. He cannot be confined to places that human-made boundaries dictate or determine. Calls often take us places we had not intended to go, had never thought we would venture, and might have preferred not to be seen in. Here, Wesley speaks to the limitlessness of God's work in us. It speaks to the dichotomous work of the Holy Spirit in us, comforting us with God's love and pulling us to places that are uncomfortable. We cannot be settled when called. We must instead go—go wherever we are being pulled to because the parish is not limited to the church. The parish is the world, and we are called to be God's love in this world.

As Wesley used it in this context, the word *vile* also intentionally shows that he was upending societal norms. In this moment, with his decision to preach in the Bristol fields, he was telling the members of the Church of England, the landed, the elite, that the poor, illiterate coal miners of lower classes were equal to those attending evensong in St. Paul's Cathedral in London. Both were worthy of God's love—equally. This was a transgressive, missionally prophetic, and, some might say, vile decision. And it was perceived as such.

When he submitted to be more vile, he preached in an area of Bristol known as the Brickfields. The crowds, used to hearing an eccentric Whitefield, were not pleased with John and, according to others in the crowd that day, "the poor man [Wesley] was pelted" after he preached.[9] In today's world, this will preach! How many times might we feel called by the Spirit to do something that we never thought we would, that might be talked about by others, or that might even get us in a bit of trouble…and it doesn't work out the way we thought it might. But the next day, undeterred, Wesley preached at Newgate Prison and the Nicholas Street Society, feeling revived after. Never give up. It's in moments like this when I can't but help think of Dory from the Pixar movie *Finding Nemo*: "Just keep swimming, swimming, swimming." Here, despite being a bit lost in his call and down and out after being pelted, John just kept preaching, preaching, preaching. And it worked.

Within three days of being in Bristol, John Wesley's entire framework of how to preach, where to preach, and what is proper versus what is missionally prophetic was wholly overthrown. This experience shook his foundational understanding of normativity, of acceptability, and replaced it with a desire to follow the spirit of God and meet the people wherever they were—even if that be on the dirtiest fields of all of England. And it's at this point in the story that I'm taken back to that day sitting in the New Room, listening to David Worthington brilliantly sum up John's action on April 2, 1739: "While John Wesley's heart may have been strangely warmed in London, it was set afire in Bristol."

Originally expecting to be in Bristol for only a bit, John ended up sticking around because the town offered a place to experiment. George had done a great job of reviving the societies, but the societies needed a bit more to really deepen their spiritual journeys. John took George's advice and gathered seven people, three women and four men, together to form bands. Within a week, two female bands and three male bands had formed. These bands were groups of four to six people, similar in age, of the same gender, and with one or two other common factors. I always say that my band would be of single moms in their late thirties who work full-time and enjoy wine. Bands were the people with whom you could be most vulnerable, the group that you could tell your struggles to and where you could go to celebrate your joys. The band leaders were expected to encourage deep spiritual development and report to Wesley the spiritual needs of people and their particular gifts and graces. As the bands developed, they therefore further shaped the religious societies, as Wesley was very responsive to the needs expressed in these smaller, more vulnerable spaces.

According to his own records (which can, at times, be a bit suspect), John preached to about fifty thousand people in his first month in Bristol. He would spend the rest of 1739 in Bristol nurturing the bands, growing the societies, and preaching five hundred sermons (only eight of which were inside church walls!).[10] It cannot be overstated how radical preaching outdoors was in this era. Of those seven OG Holy Clubbers who came together to make a pact to reform the Church of England on New Year's Eve 1738, only three would ever dare preach outdoors (with two of those being John Wesley and George Whitefield). The rest believed it would harm their goal; for how could they proceed to reform the Church of England if they were cast out of it? Suspicions around John's actions in Bristol grew, becoming more of a national concern as his societies and bands began to express their newfound faith, sometimes in distressing ways. G. M. Best recorded one of the first troubling incidents, which occurred on April 17, 1739, when John preached to the Back Lane Society. So many people crowded into one room that the floor beneath them collapsed. I guess preaching in a field wouldn't have *that* problem! Other rumors spread as people had dramatic physical reactions to his preaching—screaming, shrieking, fainting.

> *Tues. [April] 17.*
> Thence I went to Baldwin-Street, and expounded, as it came in course, the fourth chapter of Acts. We then called upon God to confirm his word. Immediately one that stood by (to our no small surprise) cried out aloud, with the utmost vehemence, even as in the agonies of death. But we continued in prayer, till "a new song was put in her mouth, a thanksgiving unto our God." Soon after, two other persons (well known in this place, as labouring to live in all good conscience towards all men) were seized with strong pain, and constrained to "roar for the disquietedness of their heart." But it was not long before they likewise burst forth into praise to God their Savior. The last who called upon God as out of the belly of hell, was I— E—, a stranger in Bristol. And in a short space he was also overwhelmed with joy and love, knowing that God had healed his backslidings.

> *Sat. [April] 21.*
> At Weaver's Hall a young man was suddenly seized with a violent trembling all over, and in a few minutes, the sorrows of his heart being enlarged, sunk down to the ground. But we ceased not calling upon God, till he raised him up full of "peace, and joy in the Holy Ghost."

Thurs. [April] 26.

While I was preaching at Newgate...immediately one, and another, and another sunk to the earth: They dropped on every side as thunderstruck. One of them cried aloud. We besought God in her behalf, and he turned her heaviness into joy. A second being in the same agony, we called upon God for her also: and he spoke peace unto her soul.... One was so wounded by the sword of the Spirit, that you would have imagined she could not live a moment. But immediately his abundant kindness was showed, and she loudly sang of his righteousness.

It does sound quite "enthusiastic." The rumors of these experiences drew more and more crowds—and more and more reactions. Charles Wesley and others tried to persuade John to discourage such reactions, fearing they would harm their efforts to remain within the Church of England, but John believed that these physical reactions were genuine responses to the work of the Holy Spirit within.

So much changed for John in Bristol—outdoor preaching, growing bands, converted souls—that it's in this town that he decided to build the first Methodist preaching house—the first Methodist building in the world. Called the New Room (appropriately named, as they had collapsed the floor of their prior gathering space), it was built in a part of Bristol called the Horsefair. It would be a physical place where the two largest societies in Bristol, Nicholas Street and Baldwin Street, could gather. Containing a chapel as well as apartments for traveling preachers, a medical dispensary, a library, and a marketplace, it was a malleable space used at the discretion of those who needed it. It was a place where people could come for any and all needs—physical, emotional, intellectual, economical, and spiritual.

However, after his time in Bristol, Wesley's reputation was tainted. He was branded a schismatic, a rabble-rouser, and a borderline dissenter. As Wesleyan historian Richard Heitzenrater declares, "His preaching was as likely to bring riots among some people as it was to bring repentance among others."[11] Those who disliked his message were known to interrupt his preaching through the ringing of bells, throwing objects at him, or herding their cows through the crowds. In the midst of this, he insisted that all are one in Christian doctrine and that beliefs do not matter—what matters are actions. He understood the Church of England to be action-less and mission-avoidant at the time—refusing to actively minister with those on the outskirts of British society. In fact, for all of the places he preached in Bristol, every morning, his first preaching stop was Newgate Prison. He chose, first, the place where those most outcast were.

So much happened in Bristol for John...and honestly for me as well. As for John, he dared to go beyond his own comfort zone and follow the Spirit of God wherever it called him; he figured out the basis of any community is a small group of people that can be vulnerable with one another; he built a versatile and adaptable community-centric space where the people dictated how it functioned and for what purpose. His message was received both poorly and well. And through all of this, he just kept going. He ignored praise and criticism and relied instead upon the Spirit of God working through him and the reactions of the people around him. He saw need and acted. He saw despair and loved. He saw people withdrawn and brought purpose and worth. *This is what it means to be Methodist.* This is the birthplace of Methodism. This is where John Wesley finally figured out what it meant to be a "brand plucked from the burning," as his mother referred to him when he was saved at the last minute from a burning parsonage. He wasn't meant to be a pulpit preacher, to conform to the standards of the Church of England. He was meant to stir up trouble, push boundaries, and love people not because they brought him money or fame in return but simply because they were also created by God and therefore worthy of love. I hope the lesson we can take from this today is clear.

We need love in this world. We need hope. But we also need a radical love that is willing to proclaim into all spaces, no matter the consequences, that God loves all and all are worthy of this love. We need radical hope to know that we can do this work because God is with us. We need the example of John getting into trouble, his reputation tainted, his official preaching authority threatened in order to truly embody the call of being Wesleyan. This identity must be reclaimed in order to move us forward as Wesleyans and as Methodists.

Discussion Questions

Have you had a Bristol moment in your life? A moment where you felt God calling you out of your comfort zone and into something new and unexpected?

What changes, both negative and positive, have you noticed in your church or The United Methodist Church more broadly since the COVID-19 pandemic and the beginning of disaffiliation? How can we, as Methodists, work to build on our strengths and confront our challenges in the wake of these events?

Is a specifically Methodist identity important to you, your spiritual life, and your church? Why or why not?

2

VILE-TALITY BEFORE AND AFTER BRISTOL

When I returned home from England, the more I contemplated Wesley's vile submission, the more I kept coming to the same conclusion: John Wesley's entire ministry was framed by a submission to be more vile. He was vile before Bristol, and he remained vile after. There was something about his call from God that pulled him toward abnormal practices, people, and principles. Bristol just so happens to be where he put in writing his own submission to be more vile. Given this, might "being more vile" be a foundational component of what it means to be Methodist? Today, is there something within Wesleyan vile-tality that we can and should reclaim?

It can be problematic to assume our modern-day labels readily apply to people in the past, but let's do the thing that we aren't supposed to do and psychologize John Wesley. Let's go all the way back to how John was raised. Now, I am not one of those types who will immediately blame mothers for the adults that their children become, but Susanna Annesley Wesley, John's mother, definitely deserves *credit* for the adult John. She might have been described as "vile" in her day, for not only was she a strong-willed woman but also a brilliant theologian. Susanna Annesley was born in 1669 into a dissenting household—which meant that her parents were not members of the Church of England. Instead, they were Puritans, a reform sect that sought to purify the Church of England of its Catholic tendencies and was thus deemed "dissenting." Puritans were known for moral and state reform, Calvinist theology, and evangelical preaching. Raised in such a household, it's no surprise that Susanna's father referred to her as a "dissenting daughter of dissent."[1] By the age of fourteen, Susanna rejected her family's Puritan tradition and joined the Church of England on her own. Five years later she married Samuel Wesley, also raised in a dissenting household, who had recently been ordained a priest within the Church of England. The two of them would conceive nineteen children (!), ten of whom would live to adulthood, including John Wesley (b. 1703) and Charles Wesley (b. 1707).

A woman before her time, Susanna famously taught her seven girls how to read before she taught them how to sew. Her parenting method, especially by today's standards, might be considered "vile." At the age of five, her children's formal education began, with her and other siblings as their main interlocutors. Play was *not* encouraged or even allowed. Her children were very serious and studious, as they were expected to be in classes for six hours each day (this is how many Puritans understood childhood and education—and is also part of the reason why the word puritanical was coined). On day one of their homeschooling, each child learned the entire alphabet (and all but two of them succeeded in this). They were taught Latin and Greek, classical studies, and theology. Despite this strict schedule (or some would say method—wink, wink), Susanna was a deeply caring mother. Unlike other mothers of her day, she sat down one-on-one with each child for a few hours on their designated day of the week. Sitting at her large wooden kitchen table, she and her kids would debate and discuss theology, philosophy, the classics, and so much more. John's (or Jacky, as she called him) day was Thursday, and Charles's day was Saturday.

Samuel Wesley, John's father, was a priest in the Church of England assigned to St. Andrew's Parish in Epworth. He was not a beloved preacher (nor a particularly good husband or father), and it was rumored that his congregants burned down his parsonage twice. In his frequent absences, he often left his associate, Inman, in charge of St. Andrew's. Susanna was not a fan of Inman, considering him a buffoon at best. Seeking to fulfill the spiritual role of being a good preacher's wife, Susanna began to hold Sunday afternoon meetings in her own home to provide some variety to Inman's monotonous message. She would read from Psalms or from one of her husband's or father's sermons. However, within a few weeks, rumors had spread of the variety and quality of preaching coming from Susanna's kitchen. To clarify, though, people at the time wouldn't have used that word, as women were not allowed to preach nor hold any sort of official authority within the Church of England. Soon, over two hundred people came to hear her, choosing her afternoon prayer meetings over the Sunday morning services. Furthermore, holding religious services outside the walls of a parish was illegal—and was reminiscent of the prior century, which was filled with religious fanaticism and civil war. While we do not have recordings of what she said or read, it is hard to believe that a woman as strong-willed and theologically-gifted as Susanna was not elaborating upon others' sermons. When her husband heard of her meetings and questioned her actions, she boldly wrote:

> If you do after all think fit to dissolve this assembly, do
> not tell me any more that you desire me to do it, for
> that will not satisfy my conscience, but send me your
> positive command in such full and express terms as may
> absolve me from all guilt and punishment for neglecting
> this opportunity of doing good to souls, when you and
> I shall appear before the great and awful tribunal of our
> Lord Jesus Christ.[2]

In other words, I'll stop what I'm doing only if you command me to and take the blame for those souls lost while you're away. Vile, indeed.

Even though Samuel was the ordained clergy of the couple, he spent most of his career writing a commentary on Job. The children did not turn to Samuel for spiritual advice but to Susanna. Letters written between her and her boys when they were at boarding school, university, and in adulthood show us the depth of theological conversation they had. On her own, Susanna wrote various meditations and commentaries on the Apostles' Creed, the Lord's Prayer, and the Ten Commandments. Her influence and brilliance cannot be overstated, and it is crucial that an updated, critical biography of her be written!

Perhaps we shouldn't blame Susanna for John's rule-bending nature but credit her for it. John was raised by a woman who pushed boundaries, who treated her sons and daughters as equals, and who managed a household while caring for a vital community. When she preached from her kitchen, John was about eight or nine years old. From his mother's example, he realized that to truly reach people, sometimes you must be willing to bend some rules and undertake some unsanctioned actions outside the church walls.

John began to play with this idea of rule-bending, questioning the norm, and *doing* church outside the parish walls during the late

1720s in Oxford. John Wesley had already graduated from Oxford and had been named a fellow of Lincoln College (a very prestigious role). His younger brother, Charles, was enrolled as a student. John was discerning where his calling was taking him—parish ministry? missions? academics? Being a fellow allowed him some flexibility, a connection to the academy, and access to pulpits when invited. After a bad internship with his father, he knew he did not want to be a parish priest. But he had a deep calling from God to change the world—after all, he was a "brand plucked from the burning"!

A bit of religious history is needed here for the rest of this story to make sense. The century prior, the English monarchy had been tossed back-and-forth between Catholic and Anglican rulers. Depending on who was on the throne, people of faith could lose rights and be jailed, killed, or expelled. All of this led to Oliver Cromwell (a Puritan) executing King Charles I, abolishing the monarchy, and ending the House of Lords, leading to a civil war. In 1649, Cromwell declared England a commonwealth and free state. He became Lord Protector of the Commonwealth and required members of Parliament to sign loyalty to him and Parliament. Under him, religious fanaticism ran rampant. Small reform and renewal groups sprang up all across England, seeking to convert people, enact reforms, and gain power. Without diving too deeply into the various monarchies after Cromwell, let's just say that because of the back-and-forth of various faiths being tolerated or persecuted, England had grown tired of religious fanatics. Parliament passed the Act of Toleration, which allowed certain non-Anglican faiths to be practiced in England so long as their adherents registered as dissenters, thus losing certain rights and status from the state (such as the right to vote and attend public university). So, in John and Charles's day, if you looked like you were out to reform the church

27

or if you were bending certain rules, or worse, if you were seemingly "enthusiastic" about faith, you might be labeled a dissenter.

Fast-forwarding to 1728, Charles Wesley is at Oxford and has begun a religious society similar to the ones his father had loved. It was a group of about five people who focused on Scripture, the sacraments, and holding one another accountable to the *practice* of faith. This small group of Oxford students quickly began to be ridiculed for their peculiar method of embracing "primitive Christianity" (the term sometimes used for the religion of the early church) and *doing* religion (as opposed to simply *believing* it). They rose early; they studied Scripture intently; they prayed incessantly; they fasted; they talked openly about their spirituality; they visited the sick; and they held each other accountable to all of this. After that disappointing internship at his father's parish, in 1729 John, being the older brother and a bit of a control-freak, took over leadership of this group. Their main characteristic quickly became centering their lives on faith as love acted out.

And, again, in eighteenth-century England—especially Oxford—this was weird. Most English citizens or Anglican people, if they went to church or were welcomed into an Anglican parish, sat down, listened to Scripture, heard a sermon, and left. There was no action required of them except filling a seat in the pews on Sunday (this might sound familiar to some of us in the twenty-first century). Even then, the privilege of going to a parish was only reserved for a select few: those who had the proper dress to enter the sanctuary, those who had geographical access or means of transportation to a parish, and those who had the luxury to take off the Sabbath from their labor. In the early eighteenth century, the idea of faith existing beyond the walls of a church was unheard of; the idea of faith being something that was *lived, acted out, embraced, embodied—that* challenged the status quo.

28

At a place like Oxford, it wasn't only the already mentioned disciplined acts of piety that made this small group weird. It was also their willingness to break the social and political norms of the day by physically (and metaphorically) going beyond the walls of Oxford to where the poor, the outcast, and the imprisoned were. This group not only breached those walls, but they transgressed the religio-political and social boundaries that determined who was deemed worthy of God's love. They began to preach to these folks, to minister with them, to ask them what their spirits needed— something the church dared not do.

John and his groupies were called many things for this peculiar way of faith before they were labeled as *Methodists*. Names such as Bible Moths (because they were attracted to Scripture as a moth is to the flame), Sacramentarians (because they advocated for frequent partaking of Communion), and the Holy Club (because it's catchy!) were tossed around to describe them—all with a derisive connotation. It's long been a question, however, of why the name Methodist was the one that stuck and where this name came from. Many historians suspect that either the term was reappropriated from a political adjective describing people who were methodical in their political stances or that it was taken from the name of a branch of Greek medical philosophy in the first century.[3] Some relate it back to Susanna's method of education, which she embedded in her children. Others look at the group's routinized, methodical way of faith and credit the etymology to that. But that's not the full story.

The earliest-known printed use of the term *Methodist* to describe Wesley and this group came in a letter printed in *Fog's Weekly Journal*, a London newspaper, in December of 1732.[4] After listing the various rules of this group, the writer goes on to state, "As these Methodists have occasioned no small stir in Oxford, so there has not been wanting variety of conjectures about them; and as several would be desirous to know our opinions of their rise, it may not be improper to acquaint you with them, which are summ'd up in these few lines of Ennius," an ancient Roman poet.[5] Translated from the Latin included in the letter, the lines read: "For they are not diviners either by knowledge or skill, / But superstitious bards, soothsaying quacks, / Averse to work, or mad, or ruled by want."[6]

There's a lot to unpack in this quotation, but for now and the purposes of this book, let's just say that in the early days of the first rise of Methodism at Oxford, this letter simply confirms that these religious folks were seen as a quirky group. There's a particular reason that the Methodists were being ridiculed publicly in 1732 Oxford, and it is referenced by the letter writer's allegation that Methodists there had caused "no small stir." In 1730, at the suggestion of William Morgan, the group began prison ministry at the county prison, the Castle, and at the city prison, the Bocardo. By 1732, most of their time was spent ministering in these places, taking "food, drink, medicines and reading matter" to those imprisoned.[7] When they saw inhumane treatment directed at those who had no other options before them, the Holy Club used their status, privilege, and education to hold the state authorities accountable. But every now and then, their actions went further, and they experimented with legal advocacy on behalf of a select few.[8] This was the case in late 1732, when an inmate named Thomas Blair "aroused Wesley's sympathy."[9]

Thomas Blair was imprisoned at the Bocardo for alleged "sodomitical practices."[10] In the eighteenth century, male-to-male intercourse or sexual acts were a capital offense. Wesley and his friend, John Clayton, believed that Mr. Blair was being victimized by his fellow inmates for his alleged crime, and they sought to ensure his protection and his humanity. Wesley "visited and read to him, made contact with the lawyer Mr. Austin and wrote out the case."[11] Letters written between Clayton and Wesley show that they took a particular interest in his trial. They "marshal'd his evidence" and sought to ensure that the case would "convince any reasonable man of his innocence."[12] The day of his trial, Wesley rose at 4 a.m. and rode twelve miles on a horse to be present. Unfortunately, Mr. Blair was found guilty in court, but his life was spared, and he was fined 20 marks. With Mr. Blair unable to raise the funds for the fine from prison, John Wesley used his connections to do so. They had done this with other prisoners, as it was part of their ministry to contribute "a tithe of their income to help pay the debts of those who were confined for relatively trivial sums."[13] It's quite telling of Wesley's embrace of those most outcast that he counted Mr. Blair as among those worthy of having their debts paid. Even after securing his release, Mr. Blair remained on Wesley's mind over the next year.[14]

Now there are many things that people take away from this story. One thing that we do know is that John Wesley and the Methodists were also deemed guilty in the public eye due to their ministry with and defense of Mr. Blair. Ignoring any potential social or other ramifications, Wesley was concerned with how Blair was being treated by others. He knew that Blair, for a crime that was reportedly "too indelicate to mention," would be targeted for multiple forms of harassment and unfair treatment. And Wesley knew *that* was wrong. To ensure that Blair felt worthy of God's love, of the love of a neighbor, and love of himself, Wesley was willing to risk all. Peter Forsaith describes this unrelenting, unconditional defense as the act of public witness that "tipped the balance between the Methodists being tolerated and being castigated."[15]

After their defense of Mr. Blair, the Holy Club was ridiculed even more for their way of doing religion—for their method that upended the norm and bent the rules by living out the love of

God through intentional outreach to those most in need and most outcast. Powerfully, Forsaith declares,

> Wesley and his Oxford friends' eccentricities might...be tolerated—their excessive religious observance, their closed group intensity, their self denial and strict code of living reminiscent of some of the wayward Puritan sects of the previous century. Even their lowering themselves to undertake good works in the prisons and workhouse was not beyond the pale. But it seems that when they took up the advocacy of a man accused of homosexual crimes they crossed the boundary between the bizarre but tolerable to the reprehensible.[16]

Today, as a person discerning what it means to be Methodist, to be United Methodist, I find it striking that we are not taught nor know this story. In case it isn't clear, the letter printed in the *Fog's Weekly* newspaper marks *the first time that the word Methodist was publicly used to describe John Wesley and his peculiar method of living out the love of God to all*. It is in doing the unimaginable, going to places unthinkable, and ministering with those outcasts that earned us the name Methodist. Perhaps, at our core, in our etymology, we are a bit "vile" indeed.

Vile After Bristol

Now that we've seen a bit of how Wesley (and some of his family) were a bit "vile" prior to 1739 in Bristol, let's see if this attitude continued. Beyond future unorthodox acts of Wesley, the people called Methodist were seen collectively as a "vile" group who embraced the countercultural spirit of primitive Christians. Scholars ascertain that "like Christians from previous historical epochs, Methodists saw themselves locked in a battle between good and evil, and they expected, perhaps even wanted, to encounter opposition."[17]

As the movement grew in followers, its reputation became even more tainted because Methodists were believed to be "enthusiastic" about their faith. This might not seem like a negative thing in the twenty-first century, but eighteenth-century England had a civil war and drastic monarchical turnover due to the political and social disputes of various religious enthusiasts (as described already in this chapter). So, "No doubt memories of the religious fanaticism associated with the civil wars of the previous century loomed large, and the Methodists were regularly compared to Cromwellian Puritans."[18] Attempting to speak to the heart, to garner a conversion moment, and to speak in a manner that uneducated people understood, John Wesley and other Methodists preached in a way that was drastically different from most Anglican preachers. They were emotional and fiery and sought to produce a reciprocal emotional response in their listeners. And they were successful; however, "The sighs, groans, and tears that became badges of honor for the heroes and heroines of sentimental fiction marked the Methodists as enthusiasts and madmen."[19] Furthermore, this reputation wasn't based only on their bodily responses to newfound or newly-revived faith but also their challenging of social and political norms. Methodists let laypeople preach; they let women preach! Both of which were strictly forbidden in the Church of England, but Wesley justified both practices as exemplary of an "extraordinary call."

The label of "enthusiasm" was often used by Methodists "as a proof of a spiritual witness that might justify social or political insubordination."[20] As Methodist historian David Hempton argues, "Methodism at its heart and center had always been a profoundly countercultural movement. It drew energy and personal commitment from the dialectics arising from its challenge to accepted norms in religion and society. It thrived on opposition, but it could not long survive equipoise."[21] Vile, indeed.

Let's look at some of the classic examples of early Methodist lore that support this. In 1742, John went to his boyhood home of Epworth to see his beloved mother. Upon arrival, he went to the St. Andrew's Parish, the church where he was baptized, confirmed, and nurtured in the Anglican faith, and he was quickly turned away. Now, by 1742, word had gotten around about how "vile" Wesley was, about how he was borderline fanatic or enthusiastic. He had become quite well known for preaching the universal love of God—for, to, and through all people no matter their class, race, education, status, or gender. And this was stirring up trouble in England. Fellow clergy began shutting the doors of their parishes, refusing to let Wesley inside the walls to preach, lest they become associated with the Methodists.

After the Sunday morning service at St. Andrew's, John spread the word that he'd be preaching that evening. Still forbidden to enter the doors of St. Andrew's, however, John looked around the parish grounds and found the one thing that he and his family owned—his father's grave. Around 6 p.m., John stepped atop his father's grave and preached his message of unconditional love, of human agency in holiness, and of walking hand in hand in the love of God despite difference. Again, he broke the rules and pushed the boundaries of society to share God's love. Vile, indeed.

Wesley constantly and consistently put people in leadership whom others or society had written off. Rather prominently, he put this into practice by placing women in leadership. Yes, he was used to seeing his mother in a leadership role, but he actually took a while to come around to women in leadership more generally, especially preaching. However, by the 1750s, Wesley was convinced that the Spirit of God falls on men and women equally. Thus, Methodism "was an area where women could find meaning outside the domestic sphere as well as within, leading many of the more educated among them to write, publish, and act in ways that transcended the limits placed on them."[22] Women speaking before men, women speaking in public outside of the home, and women claiming some sort of individual voice (independent of their husbands or fathers) "led to accusations from those hostile to the revival that Methodism disrupted family life and even that it encouraged sexual license because of their lengthy meetings that included both men and women, especially the love feasts."[23] Like John's submission and Susanna's dedication, the call of these women, their stepping outside of their so-called "proper place," was not of their own volition but was their following an often unrelenting call from God. They, too, were submitting to be more vile.

I want to highlight the ministries of two women as examples of not only how they pushed the boundaries of their gender but also how, even despite their gender, Wesley's placement of them in positions of authority was out of the norm. The first is Sarah Ryan, who served as housekeeper of the New Room in Bristol. The New Room was one of the main centers of early Methodism, and the role of housekeeper was not limited to housework. Back then, a housekeeper was a manager, in charge of all hospitality for those staying at the New Room. And they were spiritual leaders, guiding the classes that gathered there. Classes were the third main type of micro-community formed by Methodists (in addition to the societies and bands already mentioned), and as they gathered each week, they created a space of vulnerability, accountability, and worship. According to Donna Fowler-Marchant, "Offering Bible study, leading worship, and organizing the devotional life of the household by prayerful example, Methodist housekeepers in Bristol, London, and Newcastle shouldered great responsibilities in their vocation of watching over their 'families' in love."[24] This role was a huge responsibility, without which Methodism would not have been able to be as hospitable as it was, nor as organized. (Side note: it would also take a very patient person to be able to assist John Wesley, a notorious control-freak, with organizing the movement.)

Sarah Ryan had been cast aside by British society, and yet Wesley appointed her housekeeper of the New Room in 1757.[25] She was married three times, all to husbands who left her without legally divorcing her, thus tainting her reputation and leaving her in legal limbo. In the eighteenth century, the legal doctrine of coverture was enforced (it was technically enforced until the 1970s in the US—thanks, RBG!). Under this regime, women did not legally exist outside of a male relationship, either to their fathers or husbands. Thus, Sarah Ryan had no legal way to divorce her husbands, who abandoned her. Without a legal identity or any rights, she had no choice but to marry again…and again. As housekeeper, she frequently corresponded with John Wesley, whose wife was often the recipient of her letters. John's wife, Molly, was incredibly jealous of Sarah and critical of her past, often calling her a "whore." But, despite all of this, John saw Sarah as a gifted leader, organized manager, and responsible housekeeper.

As Methodism grew and challenged social norms (particularly gender norms), Methodist women "began to envision family in terms of…friendships with other Methodists rather than defined by…former ties to mother, father, and siblings, and even replacing…family of origin with new mothers, sisters, and brothers."[26] Instead of relying upon one's biological family, one's church family, band, or class became their primary familial circle. This tradition carried forth into Methodism in the Americas.[27]

Another woman who found herself in a leadership was Sarah Crosby, a Quaker by birth who converted to Methodism, preferring

George Whitefield or Charles Wesley's preaching to John's (going so far as to describe John as preaching "with no power").[28] Crosby quickly became a spiritual guide for many women, meeting with them one-on-one. However, following Mrs. Dobinson to the town of Derby, she assisted in beginning a new Methodist society in 1759. Unable to speak one-on-one to the twenty-seven people who showed up to the first meeting, Sarah chose to speak to all of them at once:

> I found an awful, loving sense of the Lord's presence, and much love to the people: but was much affected both in body and soul. I was not sure if it was right for me to exhort in so public a manner, and yet I saw it impracticable to meet all these people by way of speaking particularly to each individual. I, therefore, gave out a hymn, and prayed, and told them part of what the Lord had done for myself, persuading them to flee from all sin.[29]

In correspondence between Sarah and John, we see the subtle ways in which John was supporting women's voices in public religious settings without explicitly acknowledging (or forbidding) their preaching.

One of the first women to receive a formal preaching license was Mary Bosanquet. She preached often and to large crowds. In the 1700s, she and Mary Ryan established Cross Hall, a Christian community that housed and educated children and destitute adults. Along with preaching and Bible study, they offered many services, including some medical care. Of her own preaching she stated,

> I am conscious how ridiculous I must appear in the eyes of many for so doing. Therefore, if some persons consider me an impudent woman, and represent me as such, I cannot blame them... Besides, I do nothing but

37

> what Mr. Wesley approves; and as to reproach thrown
> by some on me, what have I to do with it, but quietly
> go forward saying, "I will still be more vile, if my Lord
> requires it"?[30]

Mary's use of the word vile here is not an intentional reference to John's 1739 submission to be more vile, but it is characteristic of the fact that this movement encouraged people to go beyond the norm. Through the leadership of John, people who were believed to be under a special or particular influence of the Holy Spirit were supported in their calls, despite institutional or social regulations that deemed it inappropriate. Prior to letting women preach or speak openly in public, John let laymen preach—and openly called it preaching. I've chosen to not focus on the preaching laymen here and instead uplift the experiences and ministries of the laywomen who spoke, exhorted, led, and preached, despite being deemed "vile" for so doing. It is through their ministries that we can see most distinctly how the vile spirit was not limited to Wesley alone.

John Wesley didn't just challenge the limitations of the church but also of the state. Later in his life, he began to reflect upon some of the deep injustices of his day. He was first introduced to the cruelty of chattel slavery on his missionary endeavor to the colony of Georgia in 1735. Upon his return home two years later, what he saw stuck with him. He was reminded of it in Bristol as the ships brought the products of the villainous institution to England. As the abolition movement was burgeoning in England, John took to writing his thoughts on paper. Using Anthony Benezet, a Quaker, as a conversation partner, John penned *Thoughts upon Slavery* in 1774. In this treatise, he condemned, in particular, the American form of chattel slavery. He called slavery out as a system, a system that deemed and degraded people from Africa as lesser, as somehow justified as property, based on no other quality except where they were kidnapped from. Furthermore, in this tract, Wesley recognized how the institution of slavery would affect Black people for generations to come, preventing them from being recognized and treated as equals for generations. Wesley argued that enslavers had deprived Africans of any and all means of improvement, and he blamed the creation of social inequalities not on Africans but on white people.

And Wesley was not just against slavery in word but in practice. When he formed the Methodist societies, according to the General Rules (which United Methodists are still called to uphold today), he did not allow enslavers to be members, and he named slaveholding as a way people actively did harm in this world. In fact, according to late Methodist historian Bobby McClain, John Wesley did not deny Sophey Hopkey, arguably his first true love and potential first marital choice, who quickly married another man (also named John), Communion solely because of his broken heart. He denied her Communion because the man she married was an enslaver, and thus, by marriage, she, too, was an enslaver.[31]

John's last letter before he died was written in February 1791 to William Wilberforce, famed British abolitionist and member of Parliament (written four days before his death on March 2). In this letter he charged Wilberforce, a Methodist, with ensuring that the people called Methodist carried on his antislavery stance and continued to fight for the dissolution of the institution, a hope that, as we'll see in the next chapter, did not carry on. The letter is printed in full below:

London, February 26, 1791
Dear Sir,

Unless the divine power has raised you up to be as Athanasius contra mundum, I see not how you can go through your glorious enterprise, in opposing that execrable villany, which is the scandal of religion, of England, and of human nature. Unless God has raised you up for this very thing, you will be worn out by the opposition of men and devils. But, "If God be for you, who can be against you?" Are all of them together stronger than God? O "be not weary in well doing." Go on, in the name of God and in the power of his might, till even American slavery (the vilest that ever saw the sun) shall vanish away before it.

Reading this morning a tract, wrote by a poor African, I was particularly struck by that circumstance,—that a man who has a black skin, being wronged or outraged by a white man, can have no redress; it being a law, in all our colonies, that the oath of a black against a white goes for nothing. What villany is this!

That He who has guided you from your youth up, may continue to strengthen you in this and all things, is the prayer of Your affectionate servant, JW.[32]

Vile, indeed.

In the last decade of his life, John submitted to what might be his most "vile" act—he assumed the responsibility of ordination, despite his not being a bishop, and ordained Richard Whatcoat and Thomas Vasey to send to the recently independent United States of America along with Rev. Dr. Thomas Coke. They were then tasked with ordaining Francis Asbury as deacon and then elder and then consecrating him as general superintendent (a process that took a whole three days). John knew this was a vile act, for he did it not inside the New Room of Bristol but behind the building, on the streets, as if it might be outside the eyes of the church there.

This action was not his last, but it is a nice bookend to his first submission to be more vile in Bristol in 1739. There was something about that town that pushed Wesley toward letting the Holy Spirit work in him in new, radical ways. When he first preached in the fields of Bristol, he found the calling for the people called Methodist: they were going to preach wherever people in need of the message of God's love were—no matter what. And one of his final acts in Bristol was letting go of the people called Methodist who had formed overseas—allowing them to split off from his beloved Church of England and thus empower them to develop independently of his control (although he did think he would retain a bit more control over them than he ended up having). From Bristol, Wesley both formed the people called Methodists and released them to become the Methodist Episcopal Church. But much to Wesley's chagrin, *those* Methodists in America wouldn't carry on his vile spirit for long: "Methodism would eventually acquire cultural and social respectability in the nineteenth century, but not until it distanced itself from the kind of spirituality that gave it its unique character in the eighteenth century. As Methodism established itself as an independent denomination, it lost something of its original identity."[33] And we'll now turn to the loss of this spirit.

Discussion Questions

What does it mean to live out or embody your faith? What would this mean for the role of the church in society?

John Wesley clearly saw a key part of his faith as going to the unloved and outcasts of society to do ministry with them. Does the church, both your own congregation and the broader United Methodist Church, effectively engage in this today? Who are the outcasts among us?

What might be different today if Methodism had not strayed from some of its key founding principles?

3

LOSING VILE-TALITY

What happened to this vile spirit? Well, after Wesley's death in 1791 and after the formation of the Methodist Episcopal Church in 1784, the movement of the people called Methodist slowly lost its vile-tality. Why? Mostly because it was no longer a movement inside of an institution; it no longer had the luxury of bending or breaking the rules—it now had the duty of making rules. And, good Lord, did Methodists make rules…and amendments to rules…and substitutions. Our *Book of Discipline* went from a cute, pocket-sized Q&A-style devotional meant to guide one on the path toward salvation and in the "method" of Methodism to a systematic lawbook, complete with trial procedures, polity that occasionally countered itself, and "big tent" ideologies that sought to hold together various theological interpretations under one large denomination.

The Methodist Episcopal Church (MEC), as the new denomination was known, suffered drastically from a drive to be seen as "respectable." Why? Because with respectability comes power. As the United States was birthed, so, too, was the Methodist Episcopal

Church. The US-centrism of our current United Methodist Church is largely due to the fact that these two institutions formed alongside one another, asking and answering the same questions, dealing with the same changes in society, and responding to similar changes in the ideology of the separation of church and state. Time and time again, when challenged, the MEC chose to abide by the state or to conform to social standards and not to do the Wesleyan thing of challenging injustices, particularly those introduced by the state or widely adopted by society. The rest of this chapter will provide examples of the various ways that Methodists, at least the leaders of the institution or the bureaucracy of the MEC, chose conformity over vile-tality.

Losing Vile-tality: Race

In 1784, the Christmas Conference in Baltimore founded the Methodist Episcopal Church, and those gathered decided to continue Wesley's stance against slavery. At the very beginning, Methodists could *not* be a member in good standing and also be an enslaver. If you were an enslaver, you were *not* given your weekly ticket to attend class meetings. You were given a strict timeline in which to manumit your slaves. But as Methodism spread through the United States, it spread the fastest in the South. And so, within six months of our founding, we began to forgo our own vile-tality for a false sense of *vitality*. Methodists compromised moral positions for numerical growth. This became more drastic in 1808 when church leaders drafted the MEC's constitution, which left it up to individual annual conferences to determine whether or not its Methodist members could be enslavers and remain in good standing. And that is when, I'm sure, John Wesley turned over in his grave. How could Methodists, those who believed in God's love and the worthiness of all people, in the ability of all people to seek the path of sanctification, of holiness, of pure love, how could *they* defend slavery?

The racism of American Methodists lived not only at the institutional level but at the local church level too. One of the first to leave the MEC because of its racist policies was a group of Black Methodists led by Richard Allen and Absalom Jones. They left St. George's Methodist Episcopal Church in Philadelphia, Pennsylvania, in 1787, after they were physically assaulted and removed from their knees while praying. In his autobiography, Richard Allen describes that morning at St. George's:

> A number of us usually attended St. George's Church in Fourth street; and when the coloured people began to get numerous in attending the church, they moved us from the seats we usually sat on, and placed us around the wall, and on Sabbath morning we went to church and the sexton stood at the door, and told us to go in the gallery.... Meeting had begun, and they were nearly done singing, and just as we got to the seats, the elder said, "let us pray." We had not been long upon our knees before I heard considerable scuffling and low talking. I raised my head up and saw one of the trustees...having hold of the Rev. Absalom Jones, pulling him up off of his knees, and saying, "You must get up—you must not kneel here." Mr. Jones replied, "Wait until prayer is over." Mr. H— M— said "No, you must get up now, or I will call for aid and I will force you away."...By this time prayer was over, and we all went out of the church in a body, and they were no more plagued with us in the church.[1]

After forming the Free African Society in 1787, Allen purchased a plot of land down the street, which was officially established as Mother Bethel Church in 1794.

45

White Methodists were determined to maintain control over the land, clergy, and members of Mother Bethel through legal efforts. Due to these unrelenting acts of white supremacy, the Free African Society eventually became a separate denomination, the African Methodist Episcopal Church (AME), in 1816, with Richard Allen as its first bishop. According to Methodist historian Dennis Dickerson, the true spirit of John Wesley's antiracism and egalitarian understanding of the world, and I would add Wesley's willingness to be vile, were carried on through Allen and the AME, not necessarily through Bishop Francis Asbury and the Methodist Episcopal Church![2]

White supremacy within Methodist ranks did not end with the mistreatment of Allen and Black Methodists in Philadelphia. Similar racist actions in New York City led to the formation of various Black congregations by 1800. Just as St. George's MEC tried to maintain white control over Black-led Mother Bethel in Philadelphia, John Street Methodist Church in New York City tried to maintain control over six Black congregations. In 1820, these six congregations founded the African Methodist Episcopal Zion (AMEZ) denomination and elected James Varick as their first bishop.[3] And any major metropolitan area in the US has similar stories; Black Methodists often left predominantly white Methodist churches due to overt racism and formed a separate congregation within a mile of the white church. So, next time you are walking around a big city—Washington DC, for example—and you see two UMC churches within a stone's throw of each other, a history of racism is probably the reason why.

Further south, Black Methodists in Charleston, South Carolina, were victims of increasing violence not only from outside the church but, by the 1830s, from within the church itself. The story of Black Methodists in Charleston is unique. John and Charles Wesley brought Methodism to Charleston in 1736—and Charleston is arguably one of the only places where Methodism (in the form of a society) continued in the colonies after Wesley's departure, predominately among the Black, enslaved population. By the time the MEC formed, Black Methodists in Charleston heavily outnumbered white Methodists. Biracial worship was the norm in the city, and this led to increasing mob violence from outsiders who were suspicious of Black enthusiasm and falsely associated it with potential insurrection. In 1785, Francis Asbury arrived in Charleston and established the first official Methodist meeting house. Its first year was the *only* year in which white Methodists outnumbered Black; it was also the only year that it was not the target of violence. By 1787, there were thirty-five white members and fifty-three Black members. Around this time, violence switched from attacks on the church property to attacks against the members themselves: "At night, while the Bishop [Asbury] was preaching, the house again crowded to overflowing, it was assailed on all sides with stones and brickbats."[4]

Throughout the 1790s, Black Methodists in Charleston had an average yearly increase of sixty-two new members, so that by 1804, there were approximately nine hundred Black Methodists, greatly outnumbering their white counterparts. With the establishment of a second Methodist church, named Bethel, many Black Methodists changed their preferred church, as its noncentral location made it less prone to direct attacks. It also offered a safer place and space for Black leadership as class leaders, exhorters, and preachers. As official abolition societies began cropping up in the 1820s and 1830s, violence became a norm for Black members, sustained from both without their congregations and increasingly so from within.

As the national conflict over slavery grew in the lead-up to the American Civil War, many white abolitionists began to dissent over the Methodist Episcopal Church's weak position on the issue. By the early 1840s, slavery had gone from a concern discussed primarily in print to one regularly preached on from the pulpit. Still, the denomination refused to take an official stance for or against slavery out of fear of losing members. Finally reaching a breaking point, those who were staunchly abolitionist in sentiment determined to leave the denomination in 1843 and formed the Wesleyan Methodist Church of America. Their inaugural *Book of Discipline* calls the MEC a "slave-defending church." Up to this point, this was the largest white group to leave the Methodist Episcopal Church in its sixty years of existence. Those abolitionists who stayed within the MEC began to ramp up their efforts and took an even stronger stance against slavery, as the disaffiliation of the Wesleyan Methodists demonstrated the ramifications of remaining neutral. (Side note: this might sound familiar to United Methodists today regarding LGBTQ+ affirmation and inclusion, lending credence the notion that history doesn't repeat itself but it sure does rhyme.)

A general conference held the next year saw the conflict over slavery come to a tipping point as Bishop James O. Andrew had recently inherited slaves through marriage. The question then shifted to, What would it mean for the denomination to maintain an enslaver as bishop? Seeing no united way forward, a "committee of nine" was formed, and it recommended that a second General Conference be held two years later in Louisville, Kentucky. Any annual conference, local church, or person that defended slavery (and wished to continue doing so) was to join that General Conference and its resulting denomination, the Methodist Episcopal Church, South.

All of these splits happened because the MEC refused to take a firm stance, grounded in its Wesleyan identity and heritage of rule-breaking and society-challenging. Instead, Methodism began to be about membership numbers, reputation, and power. And when you let these three secular ideological constructs drive the conversation, the mission of a church becomes fruitless. The lesson for today should be quite clear from this illustration. But the question remains, Are United Methodists today brave enough to finally take a firm stance and proclaim our rootedness in the full inclusion and affirmation of those outcast by society?

After the death of Francis Asbury in 1816, the Wesleyan spirit of dissent largely vanished. Under the leadership of Nathan Bangs (who was, oddly enough, not a bishop but head of the Methodist Book Concern, the denomination's publishing arm) and others, bottom-up empowerment clashed with top-down control. Methodists began to lose their willingness to be ridiculed, to be called-out, to challenge society—instead, they began to build brick churches, settled down, appealed to established society, disempowered women, and continued to silence Black members. Time and time again, Methodists chose bricks over bodies, dollars over doctrine, and the mainstream over outskirts. We failed to take strong social or political stances out of fear that they might damage our newly esteemed reputation. And this desire to be "respected" (that is, large and powerful) only grew across the nineteenth and twentieth centuries.

The debate on slavery continued, and with the conclusion of the 1844 General Conference, the MEC divided into a northern (MEC) and southern church (MEC, South). They split because they had forgotten that being Methodist means sticking out, challenging norms, being ridiculed for inclusion.

And Methodists forgot this again in 1939 when those branches merged back together to form The Methodist Church (TMC). In this merger, TMC not only conformed to social expectations but went so far as to condone institutional segregation. Five geographical jurisdictions were created, which divided up Methodists in the United States by region....at least white Methodists. All Black Methodists, no matter their geographic location, were placed in the separate, racially segregated Central Jurisdiction. Once again, we forgot our core identity of challenging norms, of doing things that make us uncomfortable, of stepping outside the status quo in order to bring the love of God and worthiness of all to the forefront. The vile thing, the truly Wesleyan thing, to do in 1939 would've been to fully integrate in the midst of a segregated Jim Crow era.

In 1968, at the insistence of the Evangelical United Brethren, the newly formed United Methodist Church dissolved the Central Jurisdiction. United Methodists entered a new phase in which many of the white members (falsely) believed that without the Central Jurisdiction, there was no longer racism or segregation in the church. If solving centuries' long systemic injustices were only that easy. According to the late Methodist historian Bobby McClain, "Ten years after the decision to dissolve the Central Jurisdiction, Grant S. Shockley and others did a wide-ranging and revealing study of the state of the church in 1976." The study concluded that "United Methodism has accepted the notion of 'inclusive fellowship' but seems unclear about the radicality of the ethics it invokes and unwilling to actualize the behavior it demands." Wow. On paper, we were bold, but in practice, we wouldn't dare be so bold. The report continued, "Guided by such a partial ethic, United Methodism over the past ten years had *identified structural desegregation with 'inclusiveness' and redistributed rather than dissolved the former Central Jurisdiction.*"[5] Again, wow. Instead of "fixing" racism through a shift in polity, it turns out that United Methodists didn't "fix" anything at all. Instead, they simply allowed the Central Jurisdiction and its accompanying racist ideologies to be absorbed into the shadows of our current polity.

Losing Vile-tality: Gender

While John Wesley empowered women in ministry and issued them preaching licenses by the 1750s, official American Methodism in the form of the MEC fell short of this inclusive vision from the beginning. This is made even more ironic considering that one of the origin stories of Methodism in America involves the actions of a committed Methodist woman. Barbara Heck, "the mother of American Methodism," immigrated from Ireland in the 1760s with her cousin, Phillip Embury. They landed in what is now Lower Manhattan. Embury had been a Methodist preacher back in Ireland but decided to become a carpenter in their new home (insert Jesus joke here). After four years in the colonies, Barbara walked in on her cousin and other men doing the absolutely most detestable thing she could think of—playing cards! Gasp! Now they were most likely not playing Go Fish, but Barbara's reaction is remarkable. She gathered up the cards in her apron and threw them in the fire! She then looked to Phillip and insisted he start a Methodist class meeting in short order. A few days later, he did. Four or five people gathered in the Embury home on October 12, 1766, for what was arguably (and staunch Metho-nerds will argue this fact) the first Methodist class meeting in America. This class meeting quickly grew and rented a space in a nearby rigging loft to meet. They then built the (arguably) first Methodist chapel, Wesley Chapel, on John Street in New York City. This structure has since been rebuilt several times but still stands as John Street United Methodist Church, which has a *fantastic* museum and story! All of this is to illustrate that without a Methodist woman literally throwing up her arms and demanding more accountability among her own family, Methodism would not yet have gotten a foothold in America.

Despite Barbara's witness, women were not permitted to officially preach within the MEC. They would eventually gain preaching licenses (1869–1880, 1920) and full ordination (1956). But a woman who Wesley would've considered gifted with an extraordinary call was officially ignored in the licensed and ordained ranks of the MEC for almost a century. In the first decades of the MEC, women who felt a call to preach either became class leaders or dared to be traveling preachers, without license or ordination and, often, with grave criticism. As Methodism grew in respectability, however, even these unofficial preachers were silenced, and thus women began to embody their calls outside the official aegis of the church.

As women so often do, they organized their own forms of ministries. They began what are typically referred to as *parachurch organizations*, which organize work that deals with the mission or vision of the church but is outside its official oversight. One of the earliest of these organizations was the Ladies' and Pastors' Christian Union, formed in 1868, which organized Methodist women into a "systematic program of home evangelistic work among the poor and neglected, under the supervision of ordained clergy."[6] Clergymen of the time had four primary purposes for these women, which can be summarized as follows: "1) to do needed work that the pastor did not have time to do, 2) to give laypeople a religious activity beyond attending church and listening to sermons, 3) to evangelize the masses—now that the 'log cabin' had given place to 'the Gothic chapel'—and 4) to develop the individuality and spirituality of the women of the church who composed 'three fourths of our members.'"[7] In other words, under white male supervision, women were empowered and organized to do the groundwork of the church—they became the church outside the walls.

52

In this way, Methodist women collectively carried the spirit of vile-tality in their ministries, but their having to do this through unofficial, unordained, unlicensed means is exemplary of the loss of vile-tality by the institution itself. Even being pushed aside, Methodist women carried on with this work. Prime examples of their "vile" ministries are evident in both the work and ministry of the Women's Christian Temperance Union and the deaconess movement. Their ministries will be affirmed in the next chapter when we examine those who sustained vile-tality.

One of the more egregious examples of how women, even when chosen as leaders, were denied by the institution occurred at the General Conference of 1888. For centuries (before Methodism was a movement), women had been included under the term laymen and other male nouns. Using this to their advantage, Methodist women began to argue that they could be elected as delegates to General Conference after the 1868 General Conference extended that right to all "laymen." Between 1872 and 1888, it was determined by various rulings that the language of "laymen" and of "he/him/his," when used throughout the *Book of Discipline*, did include women, particularly when referencing the work of "stewards, class-leaders, and Sunday-school superintendents," for the male pronoun "shall not be construed as to exclude women from such offices."[8] During the 1870s, women gained representation at certain levels of the church, leveraging their inclusion in the category of "laymen," and they eventually became members of the quarterly conferences, from which lay delegates to General Conference were chosen.

In 1888, the inclusion of women at the highest body of the church was tested. Five women were elected as "laymen" to the General Conference: Angie F. Newman (Nebraska), Mary Clarke Nind (Minnesota), Amanda C. Rippey (Kansas), Lizzie D. Van

Kirk (Pittsburgh), and Frances E. Willard (Rock River [Illinois]). These women were all active in parachurch ministries.

Many United Methodists today know that in the lead-up to General Conference, everyone seems to have an opinion and seeks to sway the delegation one way or another. Turns out this is not a new phenomenon. In the lead-up to the 1888 General Conference, many of those who opposed the election of these five women began a smear campaign. Before the official roll call and seating of delegates at the conference, the MEC bishops in their episcopal address argued that "the five women could not be seated because their eligibility as delegates had not been properly determined according to the constitutionality of the MEC."[9] While a subcommittee debated this question, the male delegates were seated and the business begun.

On May 2, 1888, the subcommittee brought its report, which stipulated that "under the Second Restrictive Rule, which was altered by the constitutional process, the church contemplated the admission of men only as lay representatives; and that as [the church] has never been consulted or expressed its desire upon the admission of women to the General Conference."[10] The subcommittee then declared that the women were neither allowed to be seated nor elected as lay delegates, and they were asked to leave. Women were allowed to be missionaries and deaconesses, to be at the front and center of Methodist witness in some of the poorest places in the world—but at the decision-making table? No.

The hypocrisy of opening up lower levels of leadership to women, including them under "laymen," and then limiting their leadership at the highest levels using the same noun is astounding and sadly unsurprising. How did we go from a movement that broke institutional rules by granting women preaching licenses in the 1750s (!) to an institution that nitpicked whether or not male pronouns included women, allowing inclusion when it demeans

54

women's identities and denying inclusion when it affirms women's leadership and participation?

Beyond this handful of stories, women continued to challenge the institution to move toward inclusion and recognition of their gifts and graces. There were moments of acquiescence, like when the MEC allowed for women to be given preaching licenses in 1869, but those were often met with ire and led to opponents of women preaching increasing their arguments against full participation and membership rights. When women sought the right to full ordination in 1880, they were heartily denied. The Committee on Itinerancy declared,

> [We] have considered the several papers referred...in relation to the licensing of women as exhorters and local preachers, their ordination, and admission to the traveling connection and eligibility to all offices in the church; and, inasmuch as women are by general consent of the Church accorded all the privileges which are necessary to their usefulness, the Committee recommends that in the respects named no change be made in the Discipline as it regards the status of women in our church.[11]

This decision of General Conference not only denied women ordination, it actually rescinded the preaching licenses granted to them for the last decade! Preaching licenses would not again be granted to women until 1920! And ordination wasn't granted until 1956, over one hundred years after the initial push for women's ordination, when The Methodist Church finally affirmed that women had the right to be fully ordained clergy and members of the annual conference in full connection. Even with ordination rights, sexism persisted, with women being sidelined from leadership positions and facing significant barriers to advancement within the church.

The conversation surrounding ensuring that women and all genders are included and protected by the constitution is still ongoing. At the 2020/2024 session of General Conference, paragraph 4 of the Constitution of The United Methodist Church saw the addition of gender and ability as protected classes. The amendment is currently up for ratification by the aggregated total of annual conference membership. And this is not the first time this has happened. In 2016, the General Conference affirmed this addition to paragraph 4, but the amendment failed in annual conference ratification, proving that misogyny still exists within our denomination. The conversation regarding women's full participation and protection within all levels of the church is not yet finished.

Losing Vile-tality: Colonialism

One of the more complicated spaces to observe our loss of vile-tality is in colonialist practices. John Wesley was not exactly against colonialism nor against the conversion of non-Christians to Christianity. However, when thinking about reclaiming the roots of our identity, it is necessary today to include Indigenous people within this conversation, for their stories are too often overlooked and untold. Methodism's involvement in colonialist practices is evident in its missionary efforts, particularly among Indigenous peoples in America. While missionaries sought to bring Christianity to Native Americans, they did so within the context of white American expansionism and exceptionalism, often bound up with the ideology of Manifest Destiny. Methodist missionaries often aligned themselves with federal policies that sought to (oftentimes forcefully) assimilate Native peoples, eradicate their cultures, and steal their land.

John Wesley was not exemplary in his position toward Indigenous people. In fact, both John and Charles Wesley were tasked by the Society for the Propagation of Christian Knowledge to travel to Georgia as voluntary missionaries to "cultivate a sense of religion among the Europeans... and if possible among the natives who for many ages have lived in the utmost darkness."[12] Charles Wesley was named by the governor of Georgia James Oglethorpe as secretary of Indian affairs. The Wesleys' misconceptions about Indigenous spiritual and cultural life were on par with those of most eighteenth-century Europeans. They assumed Indigenous people to be lesser than simply because they were not Christian and had different understandings of family, of earth, and of spirituality. Upon arrival in Georgia, before fully moving from living on the ship to the land, the Wesleys met with a few leaders of the Creeks, who warned them to not approach the Creeks in the same manner as the French or Spanish (i.e., forced conversion). Throughout his time in Georgia, John continued to write on how he wished to preach amongst the nations, particularly the Choctaws, for he considered them "the least polished, that is, the least corrupted, of all the Indian nations."

Wesley frequently referred to Indigenous people as "gluttons, drunkards, thieves, dissemblers, liars," all playing into the colonial mindset. Without having any substantial time with leaders or people, Wesley concluded that the Creeks "show no inclination to learn anything, but least of all Christianity; being full as opinionated of their own parts and wisdom as either modern Chinese or ancient Roman."[13] It is highly important to note that all of the above was written even without John Wesley meeting with a large group of Indigenous people from any nation. Due to internal politics, both between the Georgia settlers and the Indigenous nations of the area, and to politics between Indigenous nations, the Wesleys never actually preached to or with Indigenous people. There are paintings that show John preaching to Indigenous people in Georgia; however, such an event never happened. Thus, when John left the colony in late 1736, he took pen to paper and let his insecure narcissism fly: "I went to America to convert the Indians; but oh, who shall convert me?" (An eye roll or fist shake is an appropriate response here.)

Over one hundred years later, Methodists carried forward the Wesleys' and Europe's misconceptions of Indigenous culture and an unsubstantiated sense of superiority. One (of unfortunately many) egregious example of this was Methodist involvement in and coordination of the Sand Creek Massacre. In 1864, John Chivington, a Methodist minister and district superintendent, led a brutal attack on a peaceful encampment of Cheyenne and Arapaho people in Colorado. The massacre resulted in the deaths of over 230 Native Americans, most of whom were women, children, and the elderly. Despite the assurances of safety given to the tribes, Chivington and his militia attacked without mercy, driven by a belief in Christian-centric white supremacy and a desire to steal Indigenous people's lands. Chivington's actions, justified by both his racist ideology and his distorted understanding of "Christian duty," left an indelible stain on the history of Methodism. John Chivington was never held accountable for this atrocity and remained clergy in good standing within the MEC. While some Methodists later condemned the massacre, the church's initial complicity in supporting figures like Chivington reflected its broader involvement in the violent colonization of Indigenous peoples in America. The massacre remains a sobering reminder of the dangers of intertwining the Christian faith with nationalism and racial superiority.[14]

Methodists were also responsible for cultural genocide through the Indian boarding school system. These schools, which were established by various Christian denominations including

Methodists, sought to forcibly assimilate Native American children into white American society. Indigenous children were removed from their families, forbidden from speaking their languages, and stripped of their cultural identities in these schools. Methodists founded and financed at least forty-two Indigenous boarding schools (this is the number identified as of fall 2024; more may have existed). Disease ran rampant at these schools; military tactics were invoked to eradicate culture (many schools were housed on former Civil War military bases); and corporal punishment was used on children.

A particularly powerful story comes from Elizabeth Jacobs Quinton, a Choctaw who, at the age of 112, told her story of growing up in a Methodist boarding school called New Hope. She described what happened when girls, who did not understand the English language, spoke Choctaw (please read this with caution, as it is graphic): "When they first started most of the children couldn't speak any English. If they talked Choctaw [the teachers] gave them a teaspoonful of red pepper for every Choctaw word they said."[15] Red pepper for each word. Can you imagine the hate that it takes to feed a child multiple teaspoons of red pepper for them trying to communicate with you in the only language they know? How could *this type of violence and harm* be done by *Methodists*! Aren't we the people of love? Aren't we the people who go above and beyond and out of our way to bring in the outcast, to stand up for the oppressed? And yet, here we were actively doing harm, actively disrespecting and physically assaulting children because they weren't Christian. It cannot be said enough that the legacy of this colonial violence continues to impact Indigenous communities today, and the Methodist Church's participation in these schools remains a deeply painful chapter in its history.

Losing Vile-tality: The Nuclear Family and Heterosexism

Early on in the Methodist movement, Methodists were known for breaking down the barriers of the nuclear family. People who joined were often disowned from their families, and this led to Methodists becoming their own "church family." They referred to one another as brothers and sisters and to leaders and preachers as mothers and fathers. They began to queer the idea of traditional family by creating their own chosen families who respected them, affirmed them, and held them accountable to a faith acted out in love. This tradition continued in the United States, at least for the first few decades (until about 1840). But, as the MEC became "respected" throughout the nineteenth-century American context, it began to focus less on breaking norms and more on conforming to them. This is nowhere more apparent than with Methodist concepts of family and marriage.

By the 1870s, Methodists were affirming the ideals of "proper womanhood" (i.e., submissive, pious, and domestic mothers and wives), Christian manhood (i.e., active males who provided for their families), and devout children. By the 1950s, Methodists began to live into this ideal in a particularly problematic way. Between 1951 and 1966, the National Methodist Conference on Family Life "centered the Methodist family as 'the hope of the world' and taught how to better the world by increasing the number and the quality" of Methodist families and family life.[16] As historian Amy Laura Hall brilliantly puts it, in the 1950s, "Many Methodist women were sufficiently preoccupied with their own families' appearance to save off a call by Jesus to live outside the suburban box.... By the time Methodism was flourishing as the postwar norm for religiosity, there were too few resources to enable the groundbreaking, ecclesial miscegenation for which Methodists should have been famous."[17] In *Conceiving Parenthood*, Hall traces Methodist women's movements as they moved from parachurch and missionary organizations back to the home, centering women's lives on what she names the "Lysol habit," an ideology that pushed women to create "an exceptionally clean, proper home, both physically and morally, which would strengthen the nation by developing equally clean and proper American citizens."[18] The classism, racism, misogyny, and heterosexism bound up in such ideological shifts ring quite loud!

One of the ways The Methodist Church sought to center families was by naming the month of May as Family Month. TMC's National Methodist Committee on Family Life began an annual competition to name one family, nominated by local congregations, as the Methodist Family of the Year. It doesn't take a genius to guess what that family looked like: white, middle class, and suburban with a mother staying home, a father working (usually for the government), and multiple children—all active in their church and all following assumed gender roles.[19] This family was put forward each May as an ideal for all Methodists to try to live up to. It completely ignored familial difference. It played directly into the increasing consumer mindset of the 1950s, equating success with spending power. And it solidified the heterosexism of Methodism for decades to come.

During this decade, the main periodical of Methodism switched from *The Christian Advocate*, which during the nineteenth century was the most widely read publication in the world, to *Together: The Midmonth Magazine for Methodist Families*. No longer were Methodists to be overly concerned with national or international news, with the speeches or opinions of well-known bishops, or with Methodism overseas. No, during the 1950s and 1960s, Methodists were to be concerned with their own little bubble, their nuclear family. And if their nuclear family didn't look or act or believe in certain ways, then *that* screamed trouble! The pages of *Together* are filled with overly idealized stories of family life, of advice for mothers, of devotionals, of missionary activities (for spreading this idea of the white, middle class nuclear family beyond national borders), and of the latest and greatest consumer technology.[20]

Across the 1960s, Methodists began to divide over many social issues, including civil rights, women's rights, and gay rights, and two extremes of Methodism emerge—one that was active in Black, women's, and gay civil rights and another that was active in maintaining the status quo. As the sexual revolutions challenged the binaries of Methodists and Americans, Methodists were both for and against this queering of society. Some Methodists embraced these liberated understandings of sexuality. They worked with the Department of Education to rewrite sexual ethics and education for public schools (and successfully made it required teaching).[21] They founded reproductive rights foundations, assisted women in need of medical care, and worked alongside the gay rights communities to redress the collective harm done (more on this in the next chapter). However, many Methodists clung to their "respectable" binary understandings of family, marriage, and sexuality.

This is nowhere more evident than in the penning of the Social Principles, particularly a paragraph on "human sexuality" presented to the 1972 General Conference. The original paragraph presented to the delegates was affirming of all people; it reached back to those deep Methodist roots and called Methodists to stand alongside those most oppressed. It reads:

> We recognize that sexuality is a good gift of God, and
> we believe that persons may be fully human only when
> that gift is acknowledged and affirmed by themselves,
> the church, and society. We call all persons to disciplines

that lead to the fulfillment of themselves, others, and society in the stewardship of that gift. Sex may become exploitive within as well as outside of marriage. We reject all sexual expressions which damage or destroy the humanity God has given us as birthright, and we affirm only that sexual expression which enhances that same humanity, in the midst of diverse opinion as to what constitutes that enhancement. Homosexuals no less than heterosexuals are persons of sacred worth, who need the ministry and guidance of the church in their struggles for human fulfillment, as well as the spiritual and emotional support of a fellowship which enables reconciling relationships with God, with others and with themselves. Further we insist that homosexuals are entitled to have their human and civil rights insured.[22]

Wow. The above was written between 1968 and 1972 by the Study Commission on Social Principles, a diverse group of United Methodists tasked with figuring out the social witness of the newly formed church during a time of immense social change.[23] I want you all to pause and read the above again. It's so powerful.

Sexuality is a *good gift of God!* Here, Methodists name that sexuality is not something to be ashamed of but is something that God gave us to bring us joy. We cannot be *fully human* without naming and embracing our sexual selves. We cannot be *fully human* without the church (!) and society (!) also naming and embracing our sexual selves. Leaning into the Wesleyan General Rules—(1) do no harm, (2) do good, (3) attend to the ordinances of God—the next sentence names that sexuality can be harmful, and it starts by naming that it can be harmful *within* marriage.

It's vital that harm is named as a possibility within marriage before outside of marriage. A brief rant, if I may. In 1972, when this is presented to the General Conference, marital rape was legal. It was still considered a wife's duty to sexually submit to her husband if he so desired. *It is not until 1993* (yep, 1993) that marital rape was outlawed nationwide. So, in 1972, stating that sex can be exploited *within* marriage was a way that United Methodists challenged the national and state laws that stated that it was not exploitive! This is a huge statement!

Continuing, the paragraph then goes on to recognize that some people have differing opinions on how sexuality enhances our humanity. Now, I'm not one to endorse rewriting history, but the study committee could have stopped with that sentence. And if it had, the paragraph probably would have been affirmed and the last fifty plus years of debating the paragraph on "human sexuality" might not have happened. But in 1972, when the American Psychiatric Association still labeled "homosexuality" as a "mental disorder," when people who loved "outside the norm" were harassed, beaten, jailed, and murdered, the United Methodist Study Committee decided to take a stand. Instead of ending the paragraph, they continued and took a bold risk, one that harkened back to John Wesley's defense of Mr. Blair. They explicitly named "homosexuals" as "no less than heterosexuals," as "persons of sacred worth," and as persons who need the warm embrace of the church. In what seems like a parallel to calling out the harm of some sex within marriage, the committee then named the harm that can be done to the "homosexual" community, and they chose, again, to call out the church and the state and plea for "human and civil rights" to be protected. This holy boldness cannot be overstated. This paragraph would have marked United Methodists choosing to reclaim their original Wesleyan identity as people who put the outcast before and above those in power, as people who risk all to affirm all, and as people who aren't afraid to stand up and stand out. It would've been a mic drop kind of moment.

But that's not how the story ended. Due to what I've heard described by those who attended the 1972 General Conference as shock and confusion at the Study Committee's proposal, not all Methodists were ready to take that bold step of reclaiming Wesley. After hours of debate (which were rampant with harmful language against queer people), United Methodists changed some of the above language, including an amendment to protect *all* human civil rights, not just those of the queer community. But the kicker was the adoption of the amendment commonly called the *incompatibility clause*. The revised paragraph on human sexuality thus ended with an additional clause that undid every word and the original intent of the study committee, which sought to stand up and stand out for all people, explicitly naming those within the queer community. The adopted clause read: "though we do not condone the practice of homosexuality and consider this practice incompatible with Christian teaching."

This clause was a cowardly moment for The United Methodist Church. Its passage was on par with that of the creation of the Central Jurisdiction in 1939 in explicitly denying who we are as Methodists, as Wesleyans. With this one move, The UMC continued down its path of "respectability." Just like in 1939, when the "vile" thing to do, the Wesleyan thing to do, would have been to stand up and out for racial *integration*, The Methodist Church chose not to. The Methodist Church chose racial *segregation*. The vile, Wesleyan thing would have been to look the Jim Crow era in the eyes and integrate, thereby challenging national and state laws head on. But we didn't. Amid the vast changes and challenges to sexuality after the 1960s, the vile, Wesleyan thing would have been to continue to affirm and explicitly name the queer community as part of God's good gift, as of sacred worth, and in need of protection. But we didn't.

After the incompatibility clause passed, it was used as a weapon to further stigmatize and punish LGBTQ+-identifying United Methodists. Over the next five decades, they were excluded from ordination and barred from marriage. Their credentials were taken, and they became the "thing" or "issue" to talk *about* but rarely to talk *to*. There are numerous books that provide the history of this harm, and I would encourage all United Methodists to read them. But for this book, I want to focus on the fact that in 1972, we had a chance to remind ourselves of who we truly are, as Methodists, to reclaim our witness of love in this world. And we didn't. We turned against ourselves. And over the next five decades, we doubled and tripled down. We actively did harm instead of obeying the General Rules, which call us to *do no harm*. Where were the Methodists who lived out their faith as love? Where were the Methodists who dared to embrace the outcast? Where was the witness of John Wesley, who defended Thomas Blair for a crime that was "too indelicate to mention"?

The United Methodist embrace of heterosexism eventually caused a breach in the denomination. As the embrace of LGBTQ+ people within the United States slowly increased, the debate within The UMC intensified. When it appeared that the incompatibility clause might be overturned, conservative United Methodists departed and formed another Methodist denomination, the Global Methodist Church, which openly states that it will continue a heterosexist understanding of family, marriage, and sexuality and falsely claims this as orthodox Wesleyanism.

Frankly, I do not understand the logic that undergirds these claims. In what world can Wesley defend a man imprisoned for "sodomy" (and pay his bail!) and not be willing to affirm his humanity, not consider him a person of sacred worth, one who should have his civil and social rights ensured? In what world can

66

Methodists queer the structure of the nuclear family and then argue that proper families look and function in a certain way? In what world can Methodists affirm the ministry and call of women and laypeople and those whom the church deemed unable to receive a call and suddenly limit the call of God, once again, to a particular category or type of person? John Wesley and the people called Methodist defended Blair, queered family life, and affirmed the call of *all* to ministry. Period. That is fact. That is history. Anything else is censored.

Conclusion

As Methodists became presidential advisors, presidents, and senators; as they became CEOs, global missionaries, and school teachers; as they had claim to more brick churches than there were post offices in the United States, they lost a willingness to make bold statements that ensured the love and grace of God was available for and to all, but especially to those who live on the outermost edges of society. In short, they lost vile-tality.

Our desire for power and respect and our obsession with membership numbers replaced any sense of who Wesley wanted us to be. Throughout the twentieth century, as the Methodist Episcopal Church became The Methodist Church and The Methodist Church became The United Methodist Church, this desire only grew. We absorbed and silenced the radicalisms of the smaller denominations we consumed. Methodist Protestants, who merged with the MEC in 1939, were forced to give up their five decades of supporting women in ordained ministry. Without the insistence of the Evangelical United Brethren, the 1968 merger that created The United Methodist Church would not have included the mandate to dissolve the Central Jurisdiction. As Methodists became United Methodists, their power only increased, their worldwide witness grew, and their membership numbers soared outside the United States. With this prestige came internal divisions, and United Methodists were repeatedly unwilling to embrace their true roots. Again and again, United Methodists have chosen power and "respect" over the core of who we are called to be. Again and again, we've refused to follow God's call and refused to submit to "be more vile."

But that's also not the whole story. For there were individual Methodists who have continuously pushed the vile spirit forward—and have usually been pushed to the side for doing so. To them is where we turn next.

Discussion Questions

It isn't unusual for groups that are initially founded by radical reformers to change over time, becoming more concerned with social respectability and maintaining power. Can you think of other examples of this? Why or how does this happen?

What is the value of examining how groups have fallen short of their ideals over their histories?

Are there ways that you think The United Methodist Church is still losing its vile-tality today?

4

THE VILE SUSTAINERS

While the Wesleyan institutions of the Methodist Episcopal Church, The Methodist Church, and The United Methodist Church lost their vile-tality, there were individuals and groups who engaged in grassroots campaigns to remind the institution of its vile nature. Often those folks were maligned during their day or were otherwise ignored or denied their requests for full inclusion. Hindsight, however, is 20/20, and today, looking back, we often praise them for their holy boldness. And yet, are we, today, willing to follow their lead? To follow a call as they did? To challenge institutions as they did? Are we willing to submit to be more vile as they were?

Sustaining Vile-tality: Race

Earlier in this book, we heard the story of Rev. Richard Allen, who, when subjected to racist acts of white Methodists at St. George's in Philadelphia, dared to walk out and begin the Free African Society, which would become the African Methodist Episcopal Church. Through his ministry and legacy, the antislavery ministry of John Wesley lived on among Methodists. And like Wesley, Bishop Allen was slow to embrace women in ministry, but he eventually did.

71

That story starts with Jarena Lee. Jarena was a free black woman born in Philadelphia who twice felt a call to preach. When she informed her Bishop Allen of her first call, he told her that the church "did not call for women preachers." Jarena was actually relieved by this information, as it removed the burden from her of becoming a religious authority, especially at a time when women were demeaned for daring to step out of their so-called "proper place." She wrote, "This I was glad to hear, because it removed the fear of the cross."[1] However, her call to ministry came again.

In her journal she recollects her second call, which came eight years later. She was listening to Rev. Richard Williams preach at Mother Bethel in Philadelphia, and, as she describes it, "He seemed to have lost the spirit....[so] I sprang, as by altogether supernatural impulse, to my feet, when I was aided from above to give an exhortation on the very text which my brother Williams had taken."[2]

She felt God's power pulsating through her, leading her to interrupt the male preacher and provide her own interpretation. In her autobiography she described the moment she finished:

> I sat down, scarcely knowing what I had done, being frightened. I imagined, that for this indecorum, as I feared it might be called, I should be expelled from the church. But instead of this, the Bishop [Allen] rose up in the assembly, and related that I had called upon him eight years before, asking to be permitted to preach, and that he had put me off; but that he now as much believed that I was called to that work, as any of the preachers present.[3]

When asked about the history of women preaching or of motherhood within the Methodist tradition or within the Christian tradition, I always include the story of Jarena Lee. She was a free Black woman living at the beginning of the nineteenth century. She felt a call to preach but knew deep down that embodying that call was dangerous, for in her mind it would mean denying her role as a mother and claiming religious authority as a Black woman. She was relieved when she was told by her bishop that she wasn't allowed to preach. But the Spirit didn't leave her. For eight years she resisted this call until she could no longer do so. And when she lived into that call, she was actually supported by the very bishop who had previously told her it was improper.

In the twentieth century, one of the larger groups to engage in anti-racist work was the Woman's Society of Christian Service (WSCS), one of many predecessors to today's United Methodist Women. At the formation of the Central Jurisdiction in 1939, the WSCS immediately began to argue for its dissolution and to challenge the white supremacist underpinnings of racial segregation. These women organized sit-ins, boycotted Jim Crow states, and by 1952 wrote a Charter for Racial Justice. Within The UMC, the Women's Division (successor to WSCS and immediate predecessor to UMW/UWF) brought the Charter for Racial Justice into the newly formed denomination, leading to its denominational endorsement by 1980 and every eight years since.[4]

In 1960, James Lawson, then not yet a "Reverend" but a student at Vanderbilt Divinity School, was arrested for beginning the sit-in movement in Nashville, Tennessee. Years before this, Lawson had held early morning classes at local Nashville churches, teaching people how to engage in acts of passive resistance. He led role-playing sessions, ensuring that those who would participate with him in the sit-ins knew the challenges and danger that they were putting their physical selves in. Lawson had previously worked in Montgomery, Alabama, on the bus boycott there and alongside Rev. Dr. Martin Luther King Jr. He brought the civil rights movement to his town of Nashville, seeking to desegregate the local lunch counters. Lawson and seventy-nine others were arrested. Lawson became a Methodist pastor by 1962 and was leading congregations in Nashville and eventually California. He was an active force for labor rights, reproductive rights, and gay rights.

When the segregated Central Jurisdiction was abolished, the new United Methodists didn't take a breath to talk about race at the institutional level. But Black Methodists organized and found ways to ensure that their presence, voice, ministry, and witness would be honored. In 1968, Black Methodists for Church Renewal (BMCR) was formed. In its own founding, there was debate as to how much change of the institutional church they could effect. But they carried forth. In 1969, Rev. Gilbert Caldwell penned an article for *The Christian Century* entitled "Black Folk in White Churches." Speaking as a United Methodist, he writes, "Thank God for my own Black Methodists for Church Renewal. I have the feeling that if these structures had not emerged a lot of us would have received 'calls' to preach in places other than the church."[5] The structures Caldwell is referencing here are Black caucuses.

It is worth taking a moment here to note that caucuses, groups that advocate for the interests of their constituents and are not subject to control by the General Conference or annual conferences, are a vital part of United Methodist witness. They are the main form of witness for people at the grassroots level. They inform the bureaucracy of what the people in the pews and the local church pulpit desire. I like to think of them as microcosms of what Wesley intended for the people called Methodist—they are the reform groups, working as those early Methodists did, to push the denomination toward a more inclusive, more affirming love of all. Methodist historian Rev. Dr. Ken Rowe often refers to caucuses as "Methodist mavericks." He argues that since the MEC was founded, there have been two rivals: the establishment and the caucus (often with multiple caucuses working with or against one another and in opposition to the establishment). Caucuses fought against slavery, for women's ordination, against "respectability," for holiness, and for and against queer people and Black inclusion. Most importantly, Rowe reminds us that

> There is something of Wesley in the caucus strain. It was Wesley's own stubborn commitment to Christian principle that led him to tinker with the structures of the Church of England and fashion fresh models of evangelism and Christian nurture. It was Wesley's impatient sense of missional emergency that led him to license lay women and men to preach and then to ordain some of them to administer the sacraments among his scattered flock in the North American colonies. Wesley was a nuisance to all bureaucrats, bishops, and complacent institutionalists who value structure over spirit, order over life, protocol over piety.... The spirit of independence carried over into many of his spiritual children.[6]

It was through the witness of caucuses like BMCR that the General Commission on Religion and Race was formed. This general commission of The UMC is tasked with ensuring that the voices of ethnic minorities are present, heard, and valued throughout the connection. Caucuses can have real change and can lead us toward a reclamation of our Wesleyan values.

Sustaining Vile-tality: Gender

While the MEC might have pushed women to the side of the pulpit and forced them to find new ways of embodying their calls, for at least the first few decades, they continued the Methodist tradition of upending some gender norms, particularly

75

those in the South. The activities and qualities they critiqued as "sinful" or "distracting" were, according to historian Cynthia Lynn Lyerly, often considered masculine: "gambling, brawling, lawsuits, horse racing, cockfighting, and dueling…drinking, fighting, and slaveholding." Lyerly argues that Methodist critique of these hyper-male characteristics positioned Methodists, particularly Methodist women, as "a challenge to men's ideological hegemony." She elaborates upon this, claiming that "to become a Methodist meant—at the least—to embrace a worldview at odds with secular masculine values."[7]

When wives sought to convert their husbands to Methodism, they thus were trying to diminish or overturn the very qualities that society considered male. By insisting their husbands not gamble, women exerted some sense of financial control when they otherwise had none. By insisting their husbands not drink, women often protected their own bodies and those of their children from potential physical, verbal, emotional, or even sexual violence. Men who converted were taught to be meek, submissive, happy, connected, and pious—many characteristics antithetical to the ideology of nineteenth-century manhood.

As always, there were some women who broke the mold and managed to establish themselves as respected voices among church authorities. Phoebe Palmer was born in 1807 in New York City and is largely considered the founder of the holiness movement, a movement that caused deep internal divisions within the Methodist Episcopal Church and spurred a few splits later in the nineteenth century (eventually leading to the founding of the Pentecostal movement). She was raised in a Methodist household and married a Methodist man in 1827.

She bore six children, three of whom survived infancy. She took the deaths of three of her infants incredibly hard and began to blame herself and her intense love of her children as the reason that they died. She convinced herself that God took away her children because she loved them more than she loved God. As a way of coping, she determined to turn everything in her life over to God. She experienced entire sanctification by laying everything on the altar of Christ in 1837, and she finally felt much needed peace. Afterwards, she began touring New York and its surrounding areas, talking about the importance of entire sanctification or this experience of a second blessing of the Holy Spirit.[8]

In the tenor of John Wesley, she took over the class meetings begun by her younger sister. These Tuesday Meetings for the Promotion of Holiness propelled Phoebe's reputation as a female evangelist, and she soon began traveling and preaching—quite the vile thing for a woman to do in the 1850s. She was known as a phenomenal preacher by all of the foremost Methodists within the MEC and within the secular realm as well. She wrote books supporting women's right to preach and on the importance of holiness.

She lived into that Wesleyan understanding of holiness as both personal and social, with these two facets inextricably bound together. She reminded people that it's not only their relationship with God that is important but that our relationship with God is dependent upon our being in relationship with others—and vice versa. In New York City she worked with the Methodist Ladies Home Missionary Society to begin the mission at Five Points, one of New York City's poorest neighborhoods. It began on the site of an old brewery as a day school for children whose parents worked in the neighborhood. It soon expanded into a kindergarten, a vocational training school, low-income housing, and a medical dispensary. When a new need was seen within the community, the Five Points mission evolved and responded. It didn't assume fixes to presumed needs; it listened to the people it sought to serve and responded in kind. This is exactly what John Wesley and those early Methodists were doing. They went out to the places and spaces where people were suffering, where people were ignored and taken advantage of; they asked them what they needed physically, emotionally, and spiritually; and then they responded.

Later in the nineteenth century, women were officially granted preaching licenses, with the first being Maggie Newton Van Cott. After years of successful evangelism, in 1869, Maggie managed to convince enough ordained white men that she had the "gifts, graces, and usefulness" for a local preacher's license. It is worth noting that Maggie, along with other women granted licenses early on, was a widow (or a single woman). Religious authority was only recognized in women who existed outside the "proper sphere" either via being a widow or remaining single. Rarely would married mothers be recognized in a public religious setting—for that was a role reserved for the husband. As a licensed local pastor, Maggie had authority within the congregation she was appointed to but was not a full member of the quarterly conference (predecessor to the annual conference). Therefore, she was not eligible for rights or to act as a representative beyond the local church.

Within a decade of receiving the right to a preaching license, two women would come forward and challenge the MEC for full ordination. Again, the "vile" nature of Wesley and early Methodism was carried forward through the persistence of those pushed to the outskirts; they reminded (almost pestered) the institution to return to its roots. Anna Howard Shaw and Anna Oliver petitioned the 1880 General Conference for full ordination rights. They both received local preacher's licenses and graduated from Boston University School of Theology. Their examination committees (predecessor to Boards of Ordained Ministry) approved both of them for full ordination, but Bishop Edward G. Andrews of the New England Annual Conference refused to ordain either of them. So they appealed to the 1880 General Conference and were denied. Anna Oliver chose to transfer to the Methodist Protestants and was quickly ordained in full connection.

Anna Howard Shaw chose to follow a different path for her call. She was born in England in 1847 and came to the United States with her family when she was young. Shaw received a preaching license in 1871, and she gave her first official sermon that same year. However, Shaw wanted more than just a preaching license—she wanted full ordination, just like the men had. In 1876, she enrolled in Boston University School of Theology, where her calling was truly tested. Because she was a woman, she was not provided with housing or board for her theological education, though the men were. As she recounts in her autobiography, on the rare occasion that "I received and responded to an invitation to preach, I never knew whether I was to be paid for my services in cash or in compliments."[9] Within a few years, however, she had piqued the interest of the Women's Foreign Missionary Society, which began to provide her a small stipend. She graduated in 1878 and was given a two-point charge in Massachusetts, two congregations that were warring with one another. Upon the refusal of the Methodist Episcopal Church to accept her for full ordination, she left and joined the Methodist Protestant Church, which had been ordaining women for about fifteen years at that point.

However, given her unfavorable appointment, Shaw again felt called to serve God in new ways. In 1883, she returned to Boston University but this time for a medical degree—even though she had no intention of practicing medicine. She graduated a few years later and had one goal in her mind: to help other women. But she knew that "neither the ministry nor medicine could help [poor women] because those efforts didn't get to the foundation of social structure." Shaw recognized that it was not lack of spirituality or health that kept women from enjoying the same lives as men—it was the prevailing systems of power and inequality. She writes,

> Around me I saw women overworked and underpaid, doing men's work at half men's wages, not because their work was inferior, but because they were women. Again, too, I studied the obtrusive problems of the poor and of the women of the streets; and, looking at the whole social situation from every angle, I could find but one solution for women—the removal of the stigma of dis- franchisement. As man's equal below the law, woman could demand her rights, asking favors from no one. With all my heart, I joined in the crusade of the men and woman who were fighting for her. My real work had begun.[10]

Shaw began using her religious gifts on the suffrage circuit— she preached for women's right to vote based in the biblical idea that in Jesus there is no male or female but all are equal. Shaw quickly became known for her rhetorical skill and her quick wit. One of my favorite examples of this came when a male minister, citing promptings from parishioners, pointedly asked her why she always kept her hair short. (To all the female clergy out there, yes, parishioners have always commented on female bodies.) When Shaw at first declined to answer, the minister pleaded for her candidness "among friends." She responded, "Well, then, among friends, I will admit frankly that it is a birthmark. I was born with short hair."[11]

Shaw may have given up the pulpit, but she constantly used her religious calling to better the world around her, and people listened. She went on to lead the National American Woman Suffrage Organization, which led ten states to legalize women's right to vote, and during WWI, President Theodore Roosevelt asked her to lead the Woman's Committee of the Council of National Defense. For this, in 1919 she became the first woman to earn the Distinguished Service Medal. She died one month after Congress passed the nineteenth amendment, which enshrined women's right to vote in the Constitution, but did not live to see its ratification into law.

Sustaining Vile-tality: Challenging Systems

Some Methodists were actively engaged in dismantling social injustices of the early twentieth century, particularly those surrounding abuse related to alcohol and labor practices. After the Civil War, alcohol consumption increased drastically. This was due in part to what we now know as post-traumatic stress and the increased availability of hard liquor (as opposed to hard cider or wine). Alcohol consumption tended to be male-centered, and Methodist women began to argue that it was the root cause of poverty and domestic abuse. The temperance movement became *the* sphere where Methodist women began to step outside of their "proper place" within the home and dare to ask for not only a public voice but a voice at the ballot box! And so much of this strategy should be credited to Frances Willard.

Frances was born in 1839 and is most known for her work with the temperance movement as president of the Woman's Christian Temperance Union. As a political genius of her day, she knew how to bring women of all classes and political leanings together for a mission. She taught women how to step out of social norms, as spiritual guardians of their homes, into the public realm and gave them the tools for social reform and change. She empowered them to own their actions in this world and taught them that no matter how small of a change, any change in the social realm that bettered the world in some way would better the world for all.[12]

Frances was raised in a New York-area Methodist family of staunch prohibitionists. This would influence her later life in a substantial way, but her early life was dedicated to advancing women's education. After graduating from North-Western Female College in Evanston, Illinois, she taught for ten years at various posts around the country before returning as president of the college, newly renamed the Evanston College for Ladies, in 1871 and immediately began to innovate the educational curriculum for those enrolled. She treated her female students no differently than the male students were at Northwestern University, which this college was associated with. She didn't limit women's education to the "softer sciences" but rather emphasized the importance of a well-rounded education for women, including subjects like science, literature, and the arts. This approach challenged traditional gender roles and expectations for women's education at the time. She encouraged her students to think critically, pursue their intellectual interests, and develop a sense of social responsibility. Many of them went on to become leaders in various fields, and some joined her in social reform efforts later in life. Her career in education ended soon after reaching its height in 1874. That year, Evanston College for Ladies merged with Northwestern and Frances became the first female dean of the women's division of a coeducational college. However, the male dean of Northwestern was her former fiancé, and the difficulties of their past caused Frances to leave that role.

She immediately joined the temperance movement, which was gaining popularity in the mid-1870s due to a new women's organization that was making its way across the nation. The Woman's Christian Temperance Union (WCTU) brought women of all ilk together to reform the nation through the regulation of liquor. By 1874, Willard was serving as the president of the Chicago chapter of the WCTU. At the first national convention of the WCTU, she was elected its corresponding secretary; in other words, she was in charge of promotion and membership training for the organization. Within five years she was named its president, owing to her reputation for pushing women out of their comfort zones and into reform.

Frances would attribute her call toward social reform to her Methodist faith. She knew that if one was Wesleyan or Methodist that one could not simply sit idly by and watch the surrounding world suffer. John Wesley focused on balancing personal holiness, or one's personal relationship with God, with social holiness, or one's relationship with neighbor. Each of these is integrally and reciprocally related to the other. For Wesley, Christianity could not be experienced in a genuine manner in isolation. Christianity requires community, and Wesleyanism or Methodism requires communal faith in action.

Willard was quite active within the Methodist Episcopal Church in the Chicago area. Her main focus was giving white women a voice at the conference table and in the pulpit. In May 1880, she attempted to address the General Conference of the MEC in order to bring greetings as the president of the WCTU (this is the same General Conference that Anna Oliver and Anna Howard Shaw petitioned for ordination). However, women were not allowed to address the General Conference, and her request caused an uproarious debate on the "woman question." This debate led Willard to coordinate educational efforts throughout the denomination on women's religious authority. She wrote *Woman in the Pulpit,* which unapologetically argued that women had an equal standing with men and should be allowed not only a voice in the denomination but full ordination rights.

In 1887 she was elected as a lay delegate to the 1888 General Conference by the Rock River Annual Conference. She was one of five women elected that year. However, when they arrived, the male delegates refused to seat them on account that they were women (see the preceding chapter for the full story). Willard and her fellow advocates did not shy away in defeat but again turned to education and advocacy. Between the 1888 and 1892 General Conferences, they used their national newspaper to advise women on how to speak with their local ministers about allowing women to enter the General Conference. They supplied them with copies of *Woman in the Pulpit* as a means to educate themselves and to give to their clergy. Their efforts continued to falter but started conversations that eventually led to women being seated as delegates in 1904.

Willard upheld the notion that "the time will come when the human heart will be so much alive that no one could sleep in any given community, if any of the group of human beings were cold, hungry, or miserable."[13] She pushed white women, particularly and specifically Methodist white women, toward a new concept of religion. One's Methodist faith should compel them to make themselves uncomfortable, to push their own boundaries, in order to spread the love of God to as many people as possible. She writes, "The religion of the world is a religion of love; it is a home religion; it is a religion of peace."[14]

For Methodist women during Willard's era, this meant speaking up and acting out. Women at this time were expected to be pious, pure, and submissive. The genius of Willard was that she took these three "ideals" and deployed them as reasons why women needed to step out of the home. If women were truly pious, then they could not sit in their homes and watch poverty, oppression, and corruption run rampant. Their faith should compel them to act in order to better the world around them—to make the world more

Christlike. And if the world really was full of sin—of social sin—this was because it was largely full of men, who were not as pure as women. So, if you want to make the world more pure, more Christlike, then women need to be active in it.

She used a rather "conservative" understanding of womanhood, particularly of Christian womanhood, to compel women to act beyond the norms of their gender. She brought women together and taught them how to be socially active. Under her leadership, the WCTU became the largest women's organization in the US. One of her first slogans was "Home Protection," and it is a wonderful example of her political genius. The Home Protection campaign was centered around the idea that alcohol abuse and the liquor trade posed serious threats to the sanctity and stability of the American home and family. The campaign encouraged women to become actively involved in the temperance movement and to advocate for prohibition as a means to protect their families. This involved lobbying for legal measures that would limit or ban the sale and consumption of alcohol. Under this slogan and its attendant political action, women could lay claim to more traditional values of womanhood while also taking public stances to influence lawmakers at the local, state, and national levels to pass temperance and prohibition laws. The Home Protection campaign also focused on education and raising awareness about the consequences of alcohol abuse. The WCTU organized lectures, rallies, and educational programs to inform the public about the social and health problems associated with drinking (some of which included egregious and false claims about the consumption of alcohol, however).

Most importantly, the Home Protection campaign taught women of the WCTU how to collaborate with other reform movements, such as women's suffrage, labor rights, and social justice, to build a broader coalition for change, and this led to her next national campaign, called "Do Everything." In her own words, a "one-sided movement makes for one-sided advocates," and thus under Do Everything women learned how systems of oppression were created and interwoven to intentionally keep women, and particularly women of color, from achieving their full potential.

The idea behind Do Everything was that any small change that a woman could make in her local context could have positive ramifications for all of women. It taught women to think locally and then consider how local change leads to regional, national, and even international change. This is representative of her efforts at getting women beyond just temperance reform to think about the right to vote, the right to work, the right to safe employment, the right to equal education, the right to own property, and a myriad of other social and political reforms. For this, Willard received a lot of pushback about teaching women "new tricks." To counter this argument, at the age of sixty, Willard learned how to ride a bicycle and then wrote a book on the newfound freedom and liberty that the bicycle afforded her. Of this experience she says, "I finally concluded that all failure was from a wobbling will rather than a wobbling wheel."[15]

For Willard, the key social sin was alcohol consumption, but the equivalent systemic sin was the lack of women's voices both in the pulpit and at the ballot box. Teaching women how to be brave enough to take small steps toward radical change at the local level was pivotal in realizing the implementation of various rights, including the right to vote. Willard's process allowed women to see that they could make a difference in the wider world. It taught them how to use their voices outside of the home for social change; it gave them a small taste of social authority. Willard would then step back and tell them how these reforms could be expanded beyond women's rights—women could help make drastic changes to labor laws, child labor in particular, to child marriage laws, to rights around healthcare and equal pay. In sum, for Willard, in her own words, "God is action—let us be like God."

Temperance wasn't the only social reform that Methodists fought for. At the beginning of the twentieth century, the Second Industrial Revolution in the US centered largely around new assembly lines and factories. This had rather dire effects on the working and living conditions in the rapidly growing and overcrowded cities. Alongside this is an increasing disparity between the haves and the have-nots, or corporate managers and factory workers. Children as young as four worked in the factories, people were paid pennies an hour, and the idea of a weekend simply did not exist. Methodists saw the overworked, underaged, underpaid, and overexposed workers and felt a need to step up and out.

By 1907, Frank Mason North, Harry F. Ward, Herbert Welch, Worth Tippy, and Elbert Robb Zaring formed the Methodist League for Social Service, which soon became the Methodist Federation for Social Service. In their first year, they drafted a social creed that focused on labor rights, calling for "the protection of the worker from dangerous machinery, occupational diseases, injuries and mortality"; "for the abolition of child labor, for such regulation of the conditions of labor for women as shall safeguard the physical and moral health of the community, for the gradual reduction of hours to the lowest practical point . . . for a release from work for one day in seven [and] for a living wage."

This creed was quickly adopted by the 1908 General Conference of the MEC, followed by the National Council of Churches, and a few years later was quoted by President Teddy Roosevelt. Remnants of its calls for labor regulations can be found in the New Deal. These original words are engraved onto a plaque in the lobby of the United Methodist Building, the only nongovernmental building to sit on

the National Mall in Washington DC, and its social witness lives on
through the General Board of Church and Society.

One of the more radical decades of Methodist social witness
and calls for legal change was the 1960s. Aside from participation
in sit-ins and witnessing against racial injustices, Methodists during
this decade fought for women's rights, specifically reproductive
rights. Methodist women, not knowing whom else to turn to, went
to the clergy (mostly male at this point) in order to receive sound
religious advice on how to continue to be intimate in their marriages
without having more children. They told stories of mental, physical,
and emotional exhaustion. They told stories of how their doctors
advised them to not have any more children, and yet they couldn't
refuse their husbands' sexual advances. During the 1960s, married
women were allowed to be prescribed contraception, but it was
rarely reliable and highly stigmatized. So, undesired pregnancies
happened, predominately among married women.

In order to assist these women, Methodist clergymen began to
network with the medical community. They created streams through
which women in need of reproductive care could receive it in safe,
sterile environments from trained, licensed medical professionals.
This was directly and explicitly in violation of state and national law.
But they continued. And they continued to the point of working
ecumenically and founding the Clergy Consultation Service on
Abortion (CCSA) in 1967. It upheld that abortion restrictions
caused "severe mental anguish, physical suffering, and unnecessary
death of women." Its goal was to "educate and inform the public to
the end that a more liberal abortion law…should be enacted" and
"to give aid and assistance to all women with problem pregnancies."[16]
In its first six months, the organization assisted and counseled eight
hundred women. By 1969, it had assisted five thousand.

The CCSA became a national network of two thousand clergy and rabbis, working together to assist women in need because national and state laws refused their bodily autonomy. Their efforts then turned to lobbying at the state level, and they were pivotal in expanding reproductive care for women across the country. After the national legalization of abortion in 1973 via Roe v. Wade, the CCSA ceased its lobbying. But The United Methodist Church recognized that full reproductive care was not entirely safe. The public rhetoric surrounding abortion was predominately negative and was also increasingly being claimed as "Christian." In order to counter that narrative and provide a different Christian understanding of reproductive care, The UMC stood up and stood out.

In 1973, with the assistance of the General Board of Church and Society and the Woman's Division, a new ecumenical gathering led to the formation of the Religious Coalition for Abortion Rights. Its sole goal was to provide a religious counternarrative to the more conservative "pro-life" rhetoric. However, it quickly became more than just a voice in public. The Coalition was called to testify before Congress in relation to the Hyde Amendment (a current law that restricts federal funding for abortion procedures) and the Human Life Amendment (a series of proposals to reverse Roe v. Wade). For this, they turned to United Methodist leaders like Theresa Hoover, who emphasized the theological aspects of questions about when life begins and the varied potential answers to those questions. Through organizations like RCAR (Religious Coalition for Abortion Rights, now known as the Religious Coalition for Reproductive Choice), United Methodists ensured that they had a voice supporting women's bodily autonomy as a God-given right and sought to protect their newly found legal right to an abortion if absolutely necessary.[17]

Another rather radical move of the 1960s was the willingness of some Methodists, particularly those in San Francisco, to stand up and stand out for the burgeoning gay movement. The previous chapter showed how The UMC reacted to the potential affirmation of queer people, but before the paragraph on human sexuality was written, some Methodists were doing the work of affirmation. In San Francisco, a handful of Methodist clergy began to recognize the harm being done to those who identified as gay. Listening to the often-Christian rhetoric employed to justify harm, harassment, and imprisonment, Methodist clergy sought to counter that narrative.

But how? What better way is there to understand a community than to go where they gather? So, under the guidance of Methodists, a handful of Protestant clergy put on their clergy collars and went to a gay bar in the Tenderloin district of San Francisco. Here, they listened. They learned of the ways that churches talked about "homosexuality," "sodomy," and other so-called "sins." They learned of how people were disowned from their families because of the Christian theologies their parents were taught. They learned of self-harm done because people were convinced that there was something wrong with them. And then they asked a crucial question: How can the church fix what it has broken?

Out of this immersive night, clergy and leaders of the gay rights movement created the Commission on Religion and the Homosexual in 1964. After a four-day ecumenical convocation in early summer brought together leaders of the gay rights movement and leaders of faith groups, the commission set its goals. They hoped to

> educate the clergy on non-heterosexual aspects of sexu-
> ality; to create opportunities for the gay community to
> educate congregations on sexuality; to continue dialogue
> between the gay community and pastors; to influence
> the nation at large on how homosexual people were tar-
> geted by law enforcement and discriminated against by
> existing laws; to encourage other denominations, clergy,

and homophile organizations to engage in dialogue; and to help the clergy understand more fully their role as pastoral counselors in a changing sexual climate.[18]

In other words, the CRH was all about radical forms of dialogue! The CRH spread modestly across the US, predominately existing in major urban areas where a gay rights movement was brewing.

One of the better illustrations of the ways that the CRH sought to create tangible change for the gay community in San Francisco occurred on New Year's Day 1965. It was the CRH's first event and first challenge. For context, it was illegal for men to dance together in public in 1964 (there were actually a surprising number of state laws regulating gender and dancing during the twentieth century—remember, *Footloose* was set in the 1980s!). In order to raise funds for the CRH, gay rights organizations of San Francisco agreed to host a drag ball as a fundraiser on New Year's Day. To assist them, the clergy worked with the police to ensure that a raid would not happen and that municipal code would be followed. However, as people arrived at the ball, they had to pass through police presence. Five hundred people were brave enough to continue walking and entered the space.

Thus, for one night, gay rights activists and clergymen and their wives danced the night away . . . but only for a few hours. That night, six people were arrested, most of them clergy who were attempting to prevent the police from entering the private event. In response to the police raid, clergy leaders of the CRH held a press conference in which they called out the police for unfair harassment and targeting of queer people. Suddenly, there was national attention on the CRH, even catching the eye of the American Civil Liberties Union. The raid on New Year's Day happened four years before Stonewall and caused a shift in the way gay rights groups organized.[19] And this is all because a handful of Methodist clergy in San Francisco walked out of their churches and into a gay bar and then dared to listen. Vile, indeed.

Conclusion

The point of this chapter has been to provide some needed hope that, even in our past when the institution failed to live up to its Methodist calling, there were individuals who heeded that call. They fought within and outside the church to live the Wesleyan witness of faith as love acted out. There were Black and white Methodists who continued to push for racial justice, fought the denomination's own racist actions and theologies, and put their own lives on the line during the civil rights movement. There were women who continued to live into their calls to ministry and embodied those calls in the pulpit, at the lecture podium, and in the public square. There were Methodists who fought to change the legal structures that created unjust and harmful systems and ideologies. Their holy boldness, their willingness to submit to "be more vile" must be named, honored, and affirmed. And truly, the stories listed in this chapter are not exhaustive by any means. I did not touch upon the witness and ministries of United Methodist Women (now United Women in Faith), nor of Affirmation, nor of the Reconciling Ministries Network, nor of the Freedmen's Aid Society, and so many more.

Discussion Questions

What commonalities do you see in the figures discussed in this chapter? What is necessary for people to take bold, prophetic action and successfully mobilize others for it?

There are many examples in this chapter of holy boldness, of living out one's faith in daring ways. How can we distinguish between this righteous kind of gospel-motivated holy boldness and simple loud brashness or extremism?

Can you think of others who have tried to go against the grain and bring a church or other organization back to its founding roots?

5

RECLAIMING VILE-TALITY

By the 1740s, Methodism had grown throughout England and those who identified as Methodists were often targets of public assault. This was the case in Wednesbury in May of 1743. The Methodist society in that town had over three hundred members. According to John Wesley's journal entries, Charles was visiting Wednesbury and accompanied the group on their four-and-a-half-mile walk to their meeting house. Being Methodist and having Charles amongst them, they sang as they walked. Upon arrival at the meeting house, they were confronted by a hostile group who shouted a quote from Acts 17:6: "Behold, they that turn the world upside down are come here also." *They that turn the world upside down.* Over their shouting, Charles stepped up on the market square (a communal marker of sorts) and preached, also from Acts. Rioters threw stones at him, and he was forced to the ground. With each attempt to regain his footing, Charles blessed those who pushed him down again.

When John heard of these riots, he recorded in his journal that it was the "zealous High-Churchmen" who "had rose up and cut all that were called Methodists in pieces." That fall, John returned to Wednesbury to preach to a peaceful crowd. Over the course of the few days there, various mobs brought John to state officials, trying to get him arrested. When unsuccessful, a mob from another town (Walsall) took control. They yelled, "Knock his brains out, down with him, kill him at once." In this particular fight, a Methodist woman stepped in and was nearly beaten to death for defending John.[1] John recorded many of the riots experienced between 1743 and 1745 in his treatise *Modern Christianity Exemplified at Wednesbury*, and from the title alone we can see that he believed the main instigators to be representatives of the Church of England.

Other riots were recorded in John's journal throughout the early 1740s, and these led him to write one of my favorite defenses of Methodism, *Advice to the People Called Methodist*. In these pages, John provided inspiration to those people called Methodist to carry on with their perceived "vile" ways. I offer it to us as inspiration to reclaim ours.

John began this treatise the way he began many, with a definition of what he means by Methodist:

> By Methodist I mean, a people who profess to pursue (in whatsoever measure they have attained) holiness of heart and life, inward and outward conformity in all things to the revealed will of God; who place religion in an uniform resemblance of the great object of it; in a steady imitation of Him they worship, in all his imitable perfections; more particularly, in justice, mercy, and truth, or in universal love filling the heart, and governing the life.[2]

In an expected manner, he continues for a few more paragraphs, essentially describing the different ways that God's love is experienced and expressed throughout *all* people's lives but clarifying that it is *only* the Methodists who embody this love in both an inward and outward fashion. He ends his long-winded definition with a call to community: "Lastly, you unite together, to encourage and help each other in thus working out your salvation, and for that end watch over one another in love, you are they whom I mean by Methodists." He then proceeds to provide *these Methodists* with five pieces of advice.

First, he advises them to "consider, with deep and frequent attention, the peculiar circumstances wherein you stand." Methodists during this time were in a bit of an odd state. They were members of the Church of England but were actively seeking to reform it from within. For this, they were being harassed and beaten by the officials and members of the Church of England. In their Methodist way of life, they began to find joy and happiness; they began to feel worthy of love of self, others, and God; and they began to form communities outside of their immediate families and the auspices of the state church. This was all quite peculiar. John lists the new particularities that he hoped they might ponder. First, "You are a new people." Methodists were new in name, in principle, and in practice. The label Methodist was new "at least, as used in a religious sense." The insistence upon holiness of heart and life, of a "peaceful, joyous love of God" and an "inward witness that we [all] are the children of God"; their "strictness of life," their method of living differently—of abstaining from "fashionable diversions," their wearing "plainness of dress," and "abstinence from spirituous liquors," among other things, such as the holding the Sabbath as holy and insisting on local, honest trade, were all new forms of living, of practice.[3]

97

How might United Methodists be new in name, principle, and practice? I don't think we are looking to rebrand or rename ourselves, but perhaps we could redefine or renew what it means to be United Methodists. And I hope that this book has encouraged you, thus far, to consider doing this through the lens of vile-tality. Perhaps we could once again be those people who *turn the world upside down*? When asked about the principles of The United Methodist Church, many of us probably think of "open hearts, open minds, and open doors." We might consider the denomination's mission *"to make disciples of Jesus Christ for the transformation of the world."*[4] But so often, United Methodists principles are not known or consistently embodied by all of its members, leaders, or clergy.

In John Wesley's day, you knew who was Methodist by their dress, their deportment, and their actions. They dressed simply, spoke plainly, avoided excess, and were generally a happy, singing people. They stuck out. Their happiness in God changed their entire countenance, and it showed. In the early nineteenth century in America, Methodists again stuck out. Some because they continued the plain dress and simple speech, but mostly they stuck out as a pain in the neck of the US bureaucracy. They challenged social and gender norms and pushed local, state, and national government to new policies of equity.

By the 1840s, however, this was gone. By the 1950s, you might only know someone was Methodist if you saw them leaving a Methodist church on Sunday morning. What happened to people being able to identify us by our very deportment, our approach to life, our love of God shining in and through us? I'm not saying here that we begin to don certain uniforms or deny our members their abilities to express themselves in whatever clothing or accessories they choose. I am wondering, though, what would it mean if someone heard you or I were United Methodist and they knew that

that faith, *that* identifier meant you were a person concerned more with social justice than social systems, that you were more concerned with reaching to those on the outskirts of society than supporting those in power, and that you were happy in God and wanted others to have the ability to find this happiness as well? What would that look like? How do we get there?

Today, we also have a chance to be new in practice. The 2020/2024 General Conference removed some obstacles and potentially opened many doorways for us. I want to prepare you for the following sentence because it's HUGE!

For the first time in our history as a connection since 1784, we are not excluding anyone from any rank or status from access to the ministries of the church!

Amazing! Imagine the possibilities that lie before us without these restrictions. We can finally live into the practice that Wesley called us to, one of a "peaceful, joyous love of God," and an "inward witness that we [all] are the children of God." And in practice, we could be new. The changes made at this most recent General Conference are so far all on paper; they have yet to be fully embodied. We adopted less US-centric language for the Social Principles, signaling a move toward decolonial principles. Slowly, across the connection, we see annual conferences, local churches, and United Methodists living into the removal of harmful language against LGBTQ+-identifying people. Those LGBTQ+ United Methodists who were defrocked are being welcomed back into the ordained fold as members in full connection. Same-gender weddings can now celebrate love without fear! And we may (fingers crossed) finally change our structure, allowing it to be distanced from its racist and colonial past and embrace a new form of equitable connection as a regionalized church. The possibilities are there. The principles have been laid before us. Are we brave enough to put these principles into practice, to submit to "be more vile," and to turn the world upside down?

This is where John's second piece of advice comes in quite handy. What he offers next, in all honesty, shocked me when I first read it. I had to pause and say each word out loud to make sure I was reading his advice correctly. Turns out I read it correctly; it's just rather stunning advice.

"Do not imagine you can avoid giving offence."[5]

Whoa. *That* advice coming from the founder and father of Methodism! He continues, "Your very name renders this impossible. Perhaps not one in a hundred of those who use the term *Methodist* have any ideas of what it means.... It is vain, therefore, for any that is called a Methodist ever to think of not giving offence."

In a remarkable rhetorical strategy, John then lists all of the ways Methodists are offensive, lining them up with the ways that they were also "new." The name, as iterated above, was offensive. Remember, in the Oxford days, the name was given as a mark of derision; it was meant to poke fun. But it stuck. And we all need to remember that perhaps *we cease to be Methodist when we forget that at first our name was an insult.* Again, I ask, What would happen if people knew what United Methodists stood for just by hearing the label?

Even more offensive than our name are our principles. John elaborates for quite a while on how offensive our principles are, so I'll do my best to sum them up. Methodists principles are offensive because we do not lay too much stress on opinions; we believe heartily in the power and inspiration of the Holy Ghost; we refrain from excess entertainment; we seek to form new types of community; we have "neither power, nor riches, nor learning; yet, with all their power, and money, and wisdom, [those opposed] can gain no ground against you." It was fully expected by John that these offensive principles might result in Methodists being cast as "madmen and fools, sometimes as wicked men, fellows not fit to live upon the earth." As a result, many Methodists might "lose, first, the love of your friends, relations, and acquaintance, even those who once loved you the most tenderly." Methodists, whose name, principles, and practices turned the world upside down were cast out because they saw the world in a way that was just too different, too equitable, too happy for many during their time.[6]

This seems a strange reason to cast people out. And I am not actually suggesting here that United Methodists be so offensive that we begin to cut off ties and relationships—that would be quite contrary to the community-centric nature of Methodism. I'm also not suggesting that we walk around just willfully angering people or being rude. However, there is something to be said for Wesley's message of being called toward offense. Methodists were "offensive" because they dared to critique those in power; they dared to see God in all people; they dared to break the standards of church, state, and society in order to allow God to work in and through all people, even to the point of letting laypeople and women preach; they critiqued slavery at the height of the Atlantic slave trade; they educated the poor and outcast; they looked at the frivolous things of this world and turned their heads away from then and toward God. Offensive? Sure. But *what an example they were of walking as Christ walked.*

Today, how can we reclaim *these* aspects of what might be called prophetic offense? Offense not for the sake of ire, or reaction, or fame, or (to use today's lingo) trolling, but offense in a future-casting way, a way that seeks to bring about the Kin-dom of God here and now. If we are to truly do that work of creating a place and space for the Kin-dom of God, we are going to have to do many things that some will consider prophetically offensive.

101

How can we critique those in power, hold them accountable for their words, actions, and policies? How can we critique the wealthy who accrue more money than is humanly possible to spend while others fight day-to-day to have their most basic of needs met? How do we protest the injustices that keep women and queer and BIPOC people from having the same rights, privileges, and status of so many who do not identify with one of those categories? How do we stand up and stand out for the lowly, the uneducated, the outcast, the anxious, the depressed? How do we turn the world upside down and submit to be a bit more vile, a bit more prophetically offensive in order to bring God's love and light into this world?

When it comes to risking what seems like all of one's securities in order to embody this offensive, vile Methodist spirit, John reminds us, with his third piece of advice, that we can depend upon God to give us the courage to do this work. Following the call of God is rarely an easy task. That's why it's a *call* and not a desire. It's never of one's own doing; it's a thing that God asks us to do on God's behalf, a way to make new rivers in the deserts and paths in the forest. Think of all those biblical characters who ran from God's call. Think back to John and his hesitancy to preach in the fields that first time. Think of those early Methodist circuit riders who jumped on horses and went headlong into the dark and unknown. Think of those early Methodist women who stepped up in front of men and proclaimed the Word of God with full authority and confidence. God is with us in those scary moments, holding one hand as we raise the other hand as a fist in protest.

Fourth, Wesley advises us to keep going and to "never rest again in the dead formality of religion" but instead "pursue with your might inward and outward holiness" God's "justice, mercy, and truth." In this fourth point, Wesley is contrasting Methodism with the "dead formality of religion" and declaring that those who hold fast to the new name, principles, and practices—even if they be offensive—have an active faith, a renewed faith. Forty years later, toward the end of his life, John wrote another treatise, *Thoughts upon Methodism*, where he expresses the exact same fear—that Methodism would continue to exist "but I am afraid, lest they should only exist as a dead sect, having the form of religion without the power."[7]

He feared this might happen if Methodists did not heed his 1745 advice after the events in Wednesbury and live out their embodied calls toward prophetic offense, trusting that God would have their backs and hold their hands as they went: "And this undoubtedly will be the case, unless they hold fast both the doctrine, spirit, and discipline with which they first set out."[8] I ask you, Have the name, principles, and practices of The United Methodist Church become one of a formal, dead faith? Are we actively seeking renewed ways to live into the love of God, without fear of offense?

And finally, Wesley advises us against complaining about the ways we suffer and the things people say against us as well as against puffing ourselves up with pride. Such grumblings and proclamations he considers "at best, loss of time; for, instead of the wickedness of men, you might be talking of the goodness of God." In speaking of the goodness of God, we recenter ourselves toward our principles and practices, focused on honing inward and outward holiness, being exemplary in the imitation of Christ so that those who speak ill might be mistaken. It doesn't take one truly involved in the nuances of The UMC to know that Methodists (of all ilk and principles) have failed in this endeavor. If you are reading this book, there's a chance that you are familiar with the inner and outer workings of the current United Methodist Church. You might be aware of the comments on social media that try to differentiate certain types of Methodism from others, that lay claim to orthodox

103

Wesleyanism, and that seek to cast aspersions on others. There are still ongoing misinformation campaigns seeking to pull United Methodists toward other expressions of Methodism, claiming that United Methodists have become too progressive or *too gay*. In all honesty, in these moments, wearing my scholar or laywoman or general secretary hat, I tend to find humor in this. I hope after reading this book that you are able to see that there is no way to look at the lives of John Wesley and those early Methodists as anything but radical.

It is impossible to say how or whether Wesley's type of radical would equate to today's progressive; every historical moment is unique. However, I can say with confidence that if John were alive today, he would critique our almost obsessive focus on which bathroom people use; our tendencies to define and limit love; our allowing billionaires to exist (and to attain national leadership positions); our relentless pursuit of material items; our forms of instant communication (i.e., social media) that oftentimes cause harm; and our unwillingness to check fact against opinion, among so many other things. Yes, the world has changed a lot since John Wesley lived, but it is still possible to reclaim the essence of what he did and stood for. And in all honesty, it shouldn't be hard.

Being Methodist is not about adhering to a set of rigid beliefs or keeping our faith confined to the sanctuary. It is about following in the footsteps of Christ, who loved so boldly and radically that it changed the world. Wesley's understanding of love was not passive; it was active, transformative, and often offensive to the status quo. In our current context, where division, fear, and injustice still plague society, we are called to reclaim this tradition of "vile" love—a love that dares to challenge systems of oppression, that welcomes all, and that refuses to exclude anyone from the table.

I've been back to Bristol once since 2022, and it still held that transformative power. A year later, I rejoined the Wesley Pilgrimage as a teacher and was given the opportunity to help lead other pilgrims through the ways we turned the world upside down. That second time being there was so similar to the first, and yet it had a profoundly different effect upon me. Between July 2022 and July 2023, I had lost both of my parents. Sitting on that same pew, singing the same songs, and hearing the same journal entries—all of it was transformative in a new way. In that year, there had been so much death, so much grief, and so many tears. In that year, I'd also begun to find a new way in the world as a single, working mom (I got divorced in June 2022, so add that to the list of stress and trauma of that year). I found my stride, balancing mom life and figuring out what it meant to be "Ashley" once again. I also took the "be more vile" obsession and worked it over and over and over, with it eventually leading to speaking and teaching sessions with the Council of Bishops, multiple annual conferences, and local churches. Hopefully some of you who have taken the time to read this history were inspired at one of those events.

I've also found a deeper understanding of love and partnership. I learned so much from my parents' relationship, especially in their deaths. We were never sure of how much my mother could understand or process after her brain bleeds. But when we told her my father had died, she turned her head, shed one tear, and the next morning her hair was a bit whiter. She knew. My dad was not perfect; my mom was almost as close to perfect as could be. But the two of them, together, strove for perfection in this world, sowing love wherever they went; they showed up, stood up, and stood out for those in need; and they taught my sister and me how to do this and why it is so important to *be Wesleyan* in this world. In death, there is life. In their deaths, I found a renewed commitment to the

Wesleyan witness. In their deaths, I found new definitions of love. In their deaths, I found a new respect for living life while we are here on earth to live it.

The United Methodist Church has experienced such trauma over the last five years. From the shock of the 2019 Special Session of General Conference, the legal battles over church property, and the sheer harmful even hateful rhetoric between so many of us, we have, in a sense, experienced a form of death. We are, at least, in a period of grieving the connection we all once knew. But still, in death there is life. In grief there can be love. How do we allow these last five years to reshape us, renew us, and call us once again to be the people that we truly are? How do we reclaim some of the rabble-rouser characteristics of John Wesley? How do we honor those who sustained the vile spirit despite the institutional church losing its identity? How do we embody the spirits of Richard, Jarena, Phoebe, Maggie, Frances, and James? One of the first steps to doing any of this work is education and getting informed. You've now been exposed to, at least, a brief history of our varied identities as Methodists. Now, it's up to you to figure out what you're going to do with the information provided. What are you going to do when God calls you next? Will you go to the new fields? Will you risk all, even if it means being a bit more vile? Are you willing to turn the world upside down? I pray that you are. If we are going to truly be United Methodist in this world, we must reclaim this type of prophetic offensive, because this world needs an organized, collective witness of love; it needs people who are willing to put their own reputations on the line for the sake of others; and it needs Methodists!

After COVID-19 and after disaffiliation, it is time for The United Methodist Church to take ownership of its history, of its story, of its identity. It is time that we tell that story over and over, for all of its beauty and so that we do not repeat our past harms. So, be ready to tell the story of the people called Methodist once more, but this time, hopefully, with a new angle on it. Perhaps that angle is "enthusiastic." Perhaps that angle is one that will turn the world upside down. Perhaps that angle is prophetically offensive. Whatever it is, may we all journey together in the rebirth of our beloved United Methodist Church and help it reclaim its Wesleyan vile-tality.

Discussion Questions

What do you want Methodists to be known for? How do you want others to recognize Methodists in their actions and ways of being?

What do you envision as the future of The United Methodist Church? What do you think is likely, and what do you think is possible?

Where do you see God's work needing to be done, either in your local church or in the wider world? Where is God calling you to submit to being more vile?

POSTSCRIPT

CHRIS HECKERT

Bristol, England—where John Wesley's ministry changed, where Ashley Boggan was inspired by the words and actions of Wesley, and where my ministry changed as well.

The first time I formally acknowledged my burnout was in a letter to my district superintendent in January 2020, requesting a sabbatical for June and July of that year. For the first five years of my present appointment, I had worked tirelessly to counter the trends of decline and aging membership affecting the broader United Methodist Church, but the challenge seemed overwhelming, even inevitable. My efforts to go above and beyond to reverse the trends were taking a deeply personal toll on my mind, body, and spirit.

By the time I recognized that I needed to take a couple months off to rest, travel, and replenish, I worried that the reprieve might be too little too late. I knew that when I returned from my sabbatical I would re-engage the same downward trend without the ability to reverse it or chart an alternative course to prevent an ultimate institutional death, which caused great anxiety.

For the past nine years, I have served at Haddonfield United Methodist Church, a flagship church in Southern New Jersey, founded in 1829, sixty years after Francis Asbury preached in the town. Known as one of the largest congregations in the conference, it has a reputation for high-quality, highly-attended programs and has planted several churches and established multiple nonprofit organizations. In 1984 the average worship attendance was over one thousand, and the adult Sunday school weekly average was 380 people. When the longtime pastor of twenty-five years and visionary leader in the denomination retired in 1996, the congregation began to rapidly lose members and programs—a trend that mirrored the larger denomination and would continue until the year I arrived.

By 2020, the worship attendance had stabilized from a free fall in the previous decade to 450 a week, but Sunday school attendance, along with other small groups and faith formation programs, were declining each year to new all-time lows. The reality was that our congregation was aging rapidly, with an average of thirty members dying per year. After serving in ministry there for five years, I had performed approximately 150 funerals and saw many more on the horizon, with most of the church's leaders and top givers entering into their seventies, eighties, and nineties.

Even though we were innovating, hiring younger staff, engaging with the community, and providing quality programs, we simply were not forming faith among emerging generations. The previous faith formation programs were neither meeting the needs of nor engaging younger people, and their decline had reached a point where they were no longer able to support our large facility or ministry infrastructure—a mathematical certainty.

While this has been the case with countless churches across the denomination, my personal struggle was with the belief that it didn't have to be that way. We still had staff, we still had financial resources, we still had many assets that would enable flourishing. We had both an incredible legacy as well as present resources that could allow us to innovate, try new things, and continue to make a meaningful impact in the local community and wider world.

The deeper issue was cultural. While there was a persistent pull toward traditional programs, like the Sunday school, that were no longer bearing fruit, we lacked an alternative model that resonated with newer or younger generations. Each effort we made to innovate for the sake of our mission was met with resistance from members committed to traditional models or a lack of interest from younger people because they did not trust that they were welcome.

At the same time, other non-United Methodist churches around us were growing, planting campuses, and innovating with cutting-edge technology, marketing, and engaging mission projects. However, their theology was rooted in traditional doctrine that perpetuated social exclusion and condemnation along moralistic lines when it came to gender, gender identity, and sexual orientation.

Attempts to learn from what these churches were doing or to implement their models of faith formation didn't work within our congregation because the theology embedded within the content was ultimately inherently colonial, racist, misogynist, and noninclusive—all antithetical to the values that are deeply important to me and to a growing core of our congregation. As I sought to find faith formation resources and models to use in order to engage younger people, I observed a trend: those with progressive theology were committed to traditional methodology, and those with traditional theology were pioneering the use of progressive methodology.

Although I doubted time off alone would help me discover new faith formation models that did not fall into this pattern, I knew that I needed rest and a change of scenery to keep myself from reaching a point where I no longer felt effective in ministry.

111

Within weeks of submitting my request, my sabbatical was approved. I began planning to attend trainings, to visit innovative churches in Europe responding to the rising tide of secularization, but the apex of my time away would be a Wesleyan Pilgrimage in the UK led by Discipleship Ministries.

As a long-time admirer of Wesleyan theology, I was thrilled at the prospect of visiting the actual sites where John and Charles Wesley fostered the early movement that would change the world. This experience promised to be the revitalizing force I needed, offering fresh insights that might help reframe my stagnant perspective on disciple-making and church decline.

However, by the time the COVID-19 pandemic settled in and the world sheltered in place, it became increasingly clear that not only would my sabbatical plans be canceled, but the accelerating decline would intensify—along with my own exhaustion and burnout. Ultimately, the pandemic would change everything.

The pandemic's most significant impact was as a cultural accelerator, propelling already existing trends forward at unprecedented speed. Denominational decline, political division, secularization, reduced volunteerism, and advances in technological adoption all progressed within months at a pace that would otherwise take decades.

The Wesley pilgrimage that was originally scheduled for 2020 would finally take place the summer of 2022, giving an even greater sense of anticipation and eagerness to engage with the history and spiritual nature of the shared experience. Like the pandemic, that pilgrimage would change everything for me. This time the change was positive, offering renewal from burnout, a glimpse into an alternative way forward for the church, as well as a bridge to a new opportunity that would provide the time and resources to develop a new model of faith formation.

While visiting John Wesley's New Room in Bristol, our pilgrimage group heard the words from Wesley's April 2, 1739, journal entry read aloud:

> At four in the afternoon, I submitted to be more vile and proclaimed in the highways the glad tidings of salvation, speaking from a little eminence in a ground adjoining to the city, to about three thousand people. The Scripture on which I spoke was this, "The Spirit of the Lord is upon me, because he hath anointed me to preach the gospel to the poor; he hath sent me to heal the broken-hearted, to preach deliverance to the captives, and recovering of sight to the blind, to set at liberty them that are bruised, to proclaim the acceptable year of the Lord."[1]

I realized then, in that sacred space, that Methodism's true birth happened through both deep struggle and adaptation. The visit to Bristol, the building of the New Room, the formation of the class meeting model, and all that would follow was not Wesley's plan. It was all a response to what was not working and to the invitation of God's spirit in the midst of it to do what was needed to get good news to those who needed to hear it the most.

Sitting in John Wesley's New Room, I found hope. It would mark the beginning of a deeper exploration into Wesley's pivotal decision to "submit to be more vile" and the profound impact this choice would ultimately have on the church and the wider world. Wesley's adapting his plans to accommodate those who gathered to hear the proclaimed word in building the New Room, his forming class meetings to meet the communal and social needs of the people, and his founding of the Kingswood School in the poor mining community were all unexpected adaptations for the sake of mission in Bristol. And yet, these efforts all became defining aspects of Methodism, reverberating for three centuries.

Sitting next to me in the New Room, also being strangely warmed by the words of Wesley's journal, was Ashley Boggan. Since 2022, Ashley and I have been in conversation about Methodist identity, mission, and particularly its method. In a forthcoming book, *Calling on Fire: Reclaiming the Method of Methodism*, we will lay out what we think is the method of Methodism and how it can be newly adapted in today's context.

This is all a direct result of the journey from my burnout and frustration over congregational aging, institutional decline, and their effects on the church to the spark of curiosity triggered by the pandemic and a spirit of hope and reconnection found during a pilgrimage to sacred Methodist sites. But perhaps most importantly, my research and learning have helped me to discover a pattern within early Methodism that is successfully being replicated in new ways and can be further disseminated and implemented in the Methodist tradition.

The methodology of John Wesley's that developed in Bristol would ultimately be replicated and multiplied, forming life-giving communities that liberated and empowered the marginalized while forming faith and eventually reforming the church. That same pattern, or "method of Methodism," can be repeated and implemented today while updating the form and content of each component to meet people where they are and to form robust faith while moving them outward to share love with others, renewing and replicating the energy of Methodism's beginnings. Keep an eye out for *Calling on Fire: Reclaiming the Method of Methodism*.

NOTES

Chapter 1: The Call to Wesleyan Vile-tality

1   G. M. Best, *The Cradle of Methodism, 1739–2017* (Bristol, England: New Room Publications, 2017), 19.

2   The evangelical quadrilateral is generally accepted amongst American religious scholars and was first proposed by David Bebbington in *Evangelicalism in Modern Britain: A History from the 1730s to the 1980s* (New York: Routledge, 1988).

3   G. M. Best, *Cradle of Methodism*, 20.

4   G. M. Best, *Cradle of Methodism*, 26.

5   George Whitefield to John Wesley, March 3, 1739, in *The Works of John Wesley*, vol. 31, *Letters VII: 1789–1791* (Nashville: Abingdon Press, 2024), 290. See also "A Collection of Letters on Religious Subjects," supplement, *Arminian Magazine*, 20 (1797): 18–19.

6   John Wesley's journals, June 11, 1739, in *The Works of John Wesley*, vol. 19, *Journal and Diaries II (1738–1743)*, (Nashville: Abingdon Press, 1990), 66–68.

7   John Wesley's journals, March 31, 1739, in *The Works of John Wesley*, 19:46.

8   John Wesley's journals, April 2, 1739, in *The Works of John Wesley*, 19:46.

9   G. M. Best, *Cradle of Methodism*, 42.

10 G. M. Best, *Cradle of Methodism*, 46.

11 Richard Heitzenrater, *Wesley and the People Called Methodist*, 2nd ed. (Nashville: Abingdon Press, 2013).

Chapter 2: Vile-tality Before and After Bristol

1   Donna L. Fowler-Marchant, *Mothers in Israel: Methodist Beginnings Through the Eyes of Women* (Nashville: Wesley's Foundery Books, 2020), 4.

2   Fowler-Marchant, *Mothers in Israel*, 31.

3   Peter Forsaith, "'…too indelicate to mention…': Transgressive Male Sexualities in Early Methodism," *Methodist Review*, 12 (2020): 64.

4   Forsaith, "too indelicate," 63; V. H. Green, *The Young Mr. Wesley: A Study of Wesley and Oxford* (London: Edward Arnold, 1961), 172.

5   *Fog's Weekly Journal*, December 9, 1732.

6   William Armistead Falconer, trans., *Cicero: "De Senectute," "De Amicitia," "De Divinatione,"* Loeb Classical Library (New York: G. P. Putnam, 1927), 369. These lines were originally written by Ennius but were only preserved via a quotation from Cicero.

7   Forsaith, "too indelicate," 65.

8   Green, *Young Mr. Wesley*, 172, 181.

9   Green, *Young Mr. Wesley*, 184; see also John Wesley's journals, October 12, 13, 16, 17, 27, 31; November 4, 7, 9, 11, 13, 14, 15, 16, 1732, in *The Works of John Wesley*, vol. 17, *Oxford Diaries* (Nashville: Abingdon Press, forthcoming).

10 Forsaith, "too indelicate," 66.

11 Green, *Young Mr. Wesley*, 184.

12 Letter from John Clayton to John Wesley, September 4, 1732, as quoted in Forsaith, "too indelicate," 65.

13 Green, *Young Mr. Wesley*, 181.

14 John Wesley's journals, February 16, 19; March 1, 29; April 16, 17; May 1; June 17, 1733, in *The Works of John Wesley*, vol. 17 (forthcoming).

15 Forsaith, "too indelicate," 65.

16 Forsaith, "too indelicate," 67.

17 Brett C. McInelly, "Raising the Roof: Hymn Singing, the Anti-Methodist Response, and Early Methodist Religiosity," *Eighteenth-Century Life*, 36, no. 2 (2012): 104.

18 McInelly, "Raising the Roof," 86.

19 McInelly, "Raising the Roof," 86.

20 McInelly, "Raising the Roof," 86.

21 David Hempton, *Methodism: Empire of the Spirit* (New Haven: Yale University Press, 2005), 201.

22 Fowler-Marchant, *Mothers in Israel*, 38.

23 Fowler-Marchant, *Mothers in Israel*, 38.

24 Fowler-Marchant, *Mothers in Israel*, 50.

25 Fowler-Marchant, *Mothers in Israel*, 51.

26 Fowler-Marchant, *Mothers in Israel*, 80.

27 Cynthia Lynn Lyerly, *Methodism and the Southern Mind, 1770–1810* (New York: Oxford University Press, 2006).

28 Fowler-Marchant, *Mothers in Israel*, 89.

29 As quoted in Fowler-Marchant, *Mothers in Israel*, 92.

30 Mary Bosanquet Fletcher, *The Life of Mrs. Mary Fletcher*, ed. Henry Moore (New York: T. Mason and G. Lane, 1840), 115–116.

31 William B. McClain, *Black People in the Methodist Church: Whither Thou Goest?* (Cambridge, MA: Schenkman Publishers, 1984).

32 Letter from Wesley to William Wilberforce, February 26, 1791, in *The Works of John Wesley*, 31:290.

33 McInelly, "Raising the Roof," 104.

Chapter 3: Losing Vile-tality

1 Richard Allen, *The Life, Experience and Gospel Labors of the Rt. Rev. Richard Allen* (Philadelphia: F. Ford and M. A. Riply, 1880), 14–15.

2 Dennis Dickerson, *A Liberated Past: Explorations in AME Church History* (AMEC Sunday School Union, 2003), 26. For a more complete history of the AME see Dennis Dickerson, *The African Methodist Episcopal Church: A History* (New York: Cambridge University Press, 2020).

3 David Henry Bradley, Sr., *A History of the A. M. E. Zion Church*, Part I, *1796–1872* (Eugene, OR: Wipf & Stock, 2020). First published 1956 by Parthenon (Nashville).

4 John Saillant, "Before 1822: Anti-Black Attacks on Charleston Methodist Churches from 1786 to Denmark Vesey's Execution," *Commonplace*, 16, no. 2. https://commonplace.online/article/before-1822/.

5 As quoted in McClain, *Black People in the Methodist Church*, 94 (emphasis added by McClain).

6 Jean Miller Schmidt, *Grace Sufficient: A History of Women in American Methodism, 1760–1939* (Nashville: Abingdon Press, 1999), 152.

7 Schmidt, *Grace Sufficient*, 153.

8 As quoted in Schmidt, *Grace Sufficient*, 215.

9 Schmidt, *Grace Sufficient*, 217.

10 As quoted in Schmidt, *Grace Sufficient*, 218.

11 As quoted in Schmidt, *Grace Sufficient*, 191.

12 As quoted in Heitzenrater, *Wesley and the People Called Methodist*, 63–64.

13 As quoted in Heitzenrater, *Wesley and the People Called Methodist*, 73.

14 If you or your congregation want to know more about Sand Creek, see Gary L. Roberts, *Massacre at Sand Creek: How Methodists Were Involved in an American Tragedy* (Nashville: Abingdon Press, 2016).

15 C. M. Whaley, "Elizabeth Jacobs Quinton, Centenarian," *Chronicles of Oklahoma*, 29, no. 2 (1951): 130.

16 Ashley Boggan Dreff, *Entangled: A History of American Methodism, Politics, and Sexuality* (Nashville: New Room Books, 2018), 105.

17 Amy Laura Hall, *Conceiving Parenthood: American Protestantism and the Spirit of Reproduction* (Grand Rapids, MI: Eerdmans, 2007), 79–80.

18   Boggan Dreff, *Entangled*, 72.

19   Boggan Dreff, *Entangled*, 72; Hall, *Conceiving Parenthood*.

20   Boggan Dreff, *Entangled*, 79–84.

21   Boggan Dreff, *Entangled*, 126–139.

22   *Daily Christian Advocate* (Nashville: The United Methodist Publishing House, 1972), 709.

23   Their entire report can be found in the *Daily Christian Advocate* (1972), 483–487.

Chapter 4: The Vile Sustainers

1   Jarena Lee, *Religious Experience and Journal of Mrs. Jarena Lee, Giving an Account of Her Call to Preach the Gospel* (Philadelphia, 1849), 11.

2   Lee, *Religious Experience*, 17.

3   Lee, *Religious Experience*, 17.

4   Ashley Boggan Dreff, *Nevertheless: American Methodists and Women's Rights* (Nashville: New Room Books, 2020), 41–51.

5   As quoted in McClain, *Black People in the Methodist Church*, 97.

6   Kenneth Rowe, "How Do Caucuses Contribute to Connection?" in *Questions for the Twenty-First Century Church*, Russell E. Richey, William B. Lawrence, Dennis M. Campbell, editors (Nashville: Abingdon Press, 1999), 243.

7   Lyerly, *Methodism and the Southern Mind, 1770–1810*, 115.

8   Schmidt, *Grace Sufficient*, 135–138.

9   Anna Howard Shaw, *The Story of a Pioneer* (New York: Harper & Brothers, 1915), 85.

10   Shaw, *Story of a Pioneer*, 151–152.

11   Shaw, *Story of a Pioneer*, 260. Notably, directly after recounting this incident, Shaw offers the following pragmatic comment, which further exemplifies the pressure for conformity: "That was the last time my short hair was criticized in my presence, but the young minister was right in his disapproval and I was wrong, as I subsequently realized. A few years later I let my hair grow long, for I had learned that no woman in public life can afford to make herself conspicuous by any eccentricity of dress or appearance. If she does so she suffers for it herself, which may not disturb her, and to a greater or less degree she injures the cause she represents, which should disturb her very much."

12   Boggan Dreff, *Nevertheless*, 16–24. I highly recommend Christopher Evans, *Do Everything: The Biography of Frances Willard* (New York: Oxford University Press, 2022).

13   As quoted in Ruth Bordin, *Frances Willard: A Biography* (Chapel Hill: University of North Carolina Press, 1986), 159. Anna Adams Gordon, *The Life of Frances E. Willard* (Evanston, Illinois: National Woman's Christian Temperance Union, 1914), 149–151.

14 As quoted in Bordin, *Frances Willard*, 159–160; and in Gordon, *The Life of Frances E. Willard*, 266.

15 Frances Willard, *Wheel Within a Wheel: How I Learned to Ride the Bicycle with Some Reflections by the Way* (New York: Fleming H. Revell, 1895), 26.

16 As quoted in Tom Davis, *Sacred Work: Planned Parenthood and Its Clergy Alliances* (New Brunswick: Rutgers University Press, 2004), 129–130.

17 Boggan Dreff, *Entangled*, 168–169.

18 Boggan Dreff, *Entangled*, 215.

19 There is a fantastic online exhibit of the CRH that has primary documents and photographs of the New Year's Day Ball. https://exhibits.lgbtran.org/exhibits /show/crh/rooms.

Chapter 5: Reclaiming Vile-tality

1 See John Wesley's journals, June 18, 1743, in *The Works of John Wesley*, vol. 20, *Journal and Diaries II (1738–1743)* (Nashville: Abingdon Press, 1991), 327. See also John Wesley, *Modern Christianity Exemplified at Wednesbury* in *The Works of John Wesley*, vol. 9, *The Methodist Societies: History, Nature, and Design* (Nashville: Abingdon Press, 1989), 132–160.

2 John Wesley, "Advice to the People Called Methodist," in *The Works of John Wesley*, 9:123.

3 Wesley, "Advice," 125–127.

4 *The Book of Discipline of The United Methodist Church—2016* (Nashville: The United Methodist Publishing House, 2016), 93 (IV.¶120).

5 Wesley, "Advice," 127.

6 Wesley, "Advice," 129.

7 John Wesley, *Thoughts upon Methodism* in *The Works of John Wesley*, 9:527.

8 Wesley, *Thoughts*, 9:527.

Postscript

1 John Wesley's journals, April 2, 1739, in *The Works of John Wesley*, 19:46.

www.ingramcontent.com/pod-product-compliance
Lightning Source LLC
Chambersburg PA
CBHW010042090426
42734CB00019B/3246